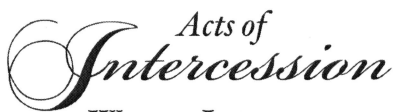

Acts of Intercession

Women Intercessors of the Bible

– A Devotional Study –

Kalamazoo, Michigan

SEASON
Press LLC

Women Intercessors of the Bible
Published by 1 Wise Choice Inc.
wisechoiceinc@gmail.com
in collaboration with Season Press LLC
Design and layout by
Fortitude Graphic Design and Printing

1. Women of the Bible – 2. Bible history – 3. Devotion
4. Motivational – 5. Self esteem

Library of Congress Control Number
2015956982

ISBN-10: 0-9863173-7-3
ISBN-13: 978-0-9863173-7-8

Published in the United States

First Edition
1 3 5 7 9 10 8 6 4 2

To my Family

Table of Contents

New Testament Women

Acknowledgments

I want to thank God the Father, God the Son–Jesus Christ, and God the Holy Ghost for giving me the insight to write this book.

Thanks to my loving husband Beauron "Ron" Wise (married 14 years as of this publication) and to my wonderful children Imani, Justin, Chris and Devon who give me daily inspiration.

Thanks to my mother, Elizabeth Hennings and my brother, William Hennings for their unconditional love and support.

Thanks to my previous pastors, Matthew Wright, Dr. J. Louis Felton and Dr. Addis Moore, and to my present Pastor Bishop Izell Kirkpatrick and Evangelist Pamela Kirkpatrick.

I am so grateful for the opportunity to write my first book. Many friends and associates encouraged me to keep writing. I took their advice and thank them for prodding me over the past seven years to accomplish my dream.

Preface

Acts of Intercession: Devotional Study of Women Intercessors of the Bible, offers an interesting and unique look into the lives and purposes of women in the Bible. Some of the women have familiar stories while others are lesser-known characters whose roles played a significant part in Bible history. Regardless of their notoriety or stature, life lessons can be learned from each of them.

After reading this book, it is my prayer that readers—especially today's women—should be able to see a glimpse of themselves in these women of the past. While the focus is on women intercessors, men also will be able to appreciate the fact that "...there is no new thing under the sun" (Eccl. 1:9).

Acts of disobedience and indiscretion were as prevalent in biblical times as they are now in the 21st Century. Ungodly, worldly sins such as stealing, lying, adultery, backstabbing, jealously, and even murder were often reasons for repentance and deliverance in biblical time. Today, increased knowledge, environmental or cultural awareness does not negate the need for continual prayer and forgiveness.

Because God gave man dominion of this earthly realm, sin will continue until the second coming of Christ. However, the contents of this book lets us know that sin does not have to consume our lives and make us feel unworthy of the redemptive blood of Jesus Christ.

We can be thankful that throughout the history God has always been and will continue to be "faithful and just to forgive our sins and cleanse us from all unrighteousness" (1 John 1:9). With this promise, it's amazing how many believers' faith is shaken or their salvation questioned when they are entangled in compromising situations and circumstances.

This seems to be especially true with many women who are often made to feel that their transgressions are larger than God's forgiveness. If you are going "through" physically, emotionally or spiritually, and you find yourself questioning everything—including God, then this book is for you.

You are not alone. Your circumstances are not unique. If you want to be in control of your own destiny, take a lesson from the women who are featured in the pages to come and see how a simple act of obedience can change your life. You will be able to understand the true meaning of "denying yourself" for the sake of others. Finally, you will be compelled to examine your current situation or lifestyle from a different perspective and feel empowered to make any necessary changes.

Reading this book has blessed me and I pray it blesses you. I pray that you are ready to walk in your purpose, use your gifts, and move forward in the name of Jesus Christ!

EDH

Introduction

This devotional was written to help women view intercession from a different angle. It was written to study the lives of the women in the Bible and allow women an opportunity to see some of the same characteristics of these women in themselves. There were many situations and scenarios that God used to get His will accomplished in earth through these women.

This book challenges you to think about where you are in life and where you are going. The ultimate goal of this book is for women to see how God can and *will* use you to get His will accomplished in earth. We are the ones who stand between heaven and earth, and we are filling the gap between the past and future generations.

We all have influence, purpose, and destinies to fulfill. My prayer is that you will find out your purpose of being more than just a woman, but an intercessor through various stories of women in the Bible. You are an intercessor and God has a tailor-made purpose just for you. Journey with me through this devotional study and start living on purpose today!

What is an Intercessor?

According to *Webster's New World Dictionary,* an **intercessor** is a person who intercedes. To intercede means to act or interpose in behalf of someone in difficulty or trouble, as by pleading or petition. It also means to attempt to reconcile differences between two people or groups; mediate.

I want to show how the concept of the act of intercession can be displayed in all of our lives. There are three types of intercession: prayers, acts, and chosen vessels.

Prayer is our direct petition unto God. It is also our personal communion with God. It may consist of request, concerns, praise and various other utterances unto Him. Intercessory prayer is defined as petitions to God for *someone else and/ or their circumstances.* It is never self-focused and is always externally focused.

Acts of obedience and/or disobedience is another avenue of intercession. It may be intentional or unintentional. We must understand that our acts can affect someone else.

Chosen Vessels are another attribute of intercession.

Before I formed you in the womb I knew you, before you were born I set you apart; I appointed you as a prophet to the nations (Jer.1: 5).

For I know the plans I have for you," declares the Lord, "plans to prosper you and not to harm you, plans to give you hope and a future (Jer. 29:11).

You did not choose me, but I chose you and appointed you so that you might go and bear fruit—fruit that will last—and so that whatever you ask in my name the Father will give you (John 15:16).

All of these verses confirm that God has a purpose and plan for all of us. All scripture was given by the inspiration of God through His prophets to reveal God's ultimate plan for our lives. All of us have been chosen to bring glory unto God. The very existence of our being means that we have been chosen for a special purpose in Christ.

Ultimately, whether intercession happens through prayer, acts, or chosen vessels, they are all used to bring glory to God through His son Jesus Christ. In the Old Testament the various women used were instrumental with the lineage and foretelling of Christ. In the New Testament the woman's role of intercession had to do with the ministry of Christ and the advancement of the early church.

The Purpose of the Woman

So the man gave names to all the livestock, the birds in the sky and all the wild animals. But for Adam no suitable helper was found. So the LORD God caused the man to fall into a deep sleep; and while he was sleeping, he took one of the man's ribs and then closed up the place with flesh. Then the LORD God made a woman from the rib he had taken out of the man, and he brought her to the man. The man said, "This is now bone of my bones and flesh of my flesh; she shall be called 'woman,' for she was taken out of man." (Gen. 2:20-23).

Our purpose as women was announced in Genesis. God had given Adam the assignment of tending to the garden and naming the animals. God saw that it was not good from man to be alone so he created woman. Why? To help Adam accomplish the assignment that God given him in the garden.

Up until this point, sin had not entered the world. Adam and his wife were equals. They were one. When he saw his wife he saw a reflection of himself. God designed man and woman to be equal partners in the ministry of establishing His kingdom on earth. Also, notice in the text that the woman did not have a name. Eve, the woman, did not get her name until sin entered the picture.

Teaching point: Do not let sin define who you are. Discovering your purpose is discovering the woman God create you to be.

The act of intercession was not needed until sin entered the world. Until that point, Adam and Eve were in perfect alignment with the Father's will. They were one with Him. But, sin created a wedge between the relationships. The woman in Genesis 3 was singled out and tempted by Satan (through the serpent), to eat the forbidden fruit from the tree of knowledge of good and evil. She ate this fruit and offered some to Adam. Once Adam ate the fruit, sin entered the world.

God had to intervene for the entire human race. The heavenly garden was violated by the act of sin. Sin cannot stand alone in the presence of God. Sin needs to be punished, covered and blotted out in His presence.

And I will put enmity between you and the woman, and between your offspring and hers; he will crush your head, and you will strike his heel (Gen. 3:15).

The Lord God made garments of skin for Adam and his wife and clothed them (Gen. 3:21).

In Genesis 3:15, 21; we see God dealing with the sin of Adam, Eve and the entire human race. This was the very first act of intercession, demonstrated through the signifying Jesus' coming to earth. This set the stage for what would be the beginning to what would lead to Jesus Christ coming to earth to die for the sins of the world. Jesus Christ is the bridge we need to get to the Father. He stands in the gap and allows us to enter into the relationship God originally intended for us to have with him in the Garden of Eden.

Intercessional covering will allow us to stand in right relationship with our Father. That is why when we pray, obey and live on purpose in the name of Jesus. He is the one who is The Intercessor of us all. Without him intercession is obsolete.

Acts of *Intercession*

Women Intercessors of the Bible

– A Devotional Study –

Shana Wise

Women of the Old Testament

Chapter 1
Sarah and Hagar

Sarah and Hagar were both chosen vessel intercessors because God used both of them to birth two great and mighty nations–the Israelites and the Ishmaelites.

Hagar

The angel of the Lord found Hagar near a spring in the desert; it was the spring that is beside the road to Shur. And he said, "Hagar, slave of Sarai, where have you come from, and where are you going?"

"I'm running away from my mistress Sarai," she answered Then the angel of the Lord told her, "Go back to your mistress and submit to her." The angel added, "I will increase your descendants so much that they will be too numerous to count."

The angel of the Lord also said to her: "You are now pregnant and you will give birth to a son. You shall name him Ishmael, for the Lord has heard of your misery. He will be a wild donkey of a man; his hand will be against everyone and everyone's hand against him, and he will live in hostility toward all his brothers."

She gave this name to the Lord who spoke to her: "You are the God who sees me," for she said, "I have now seen the One who sees me." That is why the well was called Beer Lahai Roi; it is still there, between Kadesh and Bered.

So Hagar bore Abram a son, and Abram gave the name Ishmael to the son she had borne (Gen. 16:7-15).

When the water in the skin was gone, she put the boy under one of the bushes. Then she went off and sat down about a bowshot away, for she thought, "I cannot watch the boy die." And as she sat there, she began to sob.

God heard the boy crying, and the angel of God called to Hagar from heaven and said to her, "What is the matter, Hagar? Do not be afraid; God has heard the boy crying as he lies there. Lift the boy up and take him by the hand, for I will make him into a great nation." Then God opened her eyes and she saw a well of water. So she went and filled the skin with water and gave the boy a drink (Gen. 21:15-19).

Sarah

Now the Lord was gracious to Sarah as he had said, and the Lord did for Sarah what he had promised. Sarah became pregnant and bore a son to Abraham in his old age; at the very time God had promised him. Abraham gave the name Isaac to the son Sarah bore him. When his son Isaac was eight days old, Abraham circumcised him, as God commanded him. Abraham was a hundred years old when his son Isaac was born to him.

Sarah said, "God has brought me laughter, and everyone who hears about this will laugh with me." And she added, "Who would have said to Abraham that Sarah would nurse children? Yet I have borne him a son in his old age."

And the LORD visited Sarah as he had said, and the LORD did unto Sarah as he had spoken. For Sarah conceived, and bare Abraham a son in his old age, at the set time of which God had spoken to him. And Abraham called the name of his son that was born unto him, whom Sarah bare to him, Isaac. And Abraham circumcised his son Isaac being eight days old, as God had commanded him. And Abraham was an hundred years old, when his son Isaac was born unto him. And Sarah said, God hath made me to laugh, so that all that hear will laugh with me. And she said, Who would have said unto Abraham, that Sarah should have given children suck? for I have born him a son in his old age (Gen. 21:1-7).

When I think about the story of Sarah and Hagar, I think about the term, "Baby Mama Drama." Baby Mama Drama is the conflict between two women who have children by the same man. There are many women who "get into it," with one another because of the results of this unintended connection. These individuals—the women and sometimes the man involved—experience feelings of pain, heartaches, jealousy, hurt, betrayal, insecurity, and the list goes on.

During the time of Sarah and Abraham, it was common for people to own slaves. In Genesis 12:1-9 God told Abraham that he would be the father of many nations. Yet Abraham and Sarah decided to help God out and take this conception issue into their own hands. They both thought that they were too old to have children so Sarah suggested that Abraham sleep with her servant/slave Hagar. Abraham agreed.

We all carry a level of influence, especially as women. We have to make sure that our earthly influence does not conflict with the word of God. If God promised us something, then we must trust that He is going to do just what He said he would. Sarah suggesting Abraham sleep with Hagar, turned into a problem instead of a solution. Sarah knew that God told Abraham that he was going to have a son of his own, but Sarah's solution to their infertility problem was not God-lead.

It reminds me of when Eve offered Adam a bite of the fruit from the tree of knowledge of good and evil in the Garden of Eden. God instructed them not to eat from the tree, but Eve used her influence, and caused Adam to sin with her. We have to be careful how we use our influence with the people God places in our lives. Influence—if not used in a Godly way—may cause us to manipulate others to conform to our agenda.

Hagar was a woman who was put into a situation that she did not ask for. She was a young Egyptian slave to Sarah from another culture than Abraham and Sarah. Because of her ability to conceive, she was forced to enter into a sexual relationship with a married man (Abraham). This was the mandated suggestion of her master Sarah. However, while Hagar began to show her pregnancy, Sarah became jealous of her and began to mistreat her. This made Hagar run away. She had a classic case of "fight or flight" syndrome. She had a habit of running away when her problems got too hard to bear.

Hagar ran away into the wilderness and that's when she discovered God.

> In Genesis 16:13 Hagar had a wonderful experience with God: And she called the name of the LORD that spake unto her: She gave this name to the LORD who spoke to her: "You are the God who sees me," for she said, "I have now seen the One who sees me."

God spoke to her with some instructions on how she was suppose to act in her master's house. She was to obey Sarah. He also made her some promises concerning her seed. He told her what to name her son, and promised that He was going to make him a great nation. Lastly, God told her about the future struggle between that nation and others. She blessed God, did as she was told, and went back to submit herself to Sarah. Hager later gave birth to Ishmael.

Ten years later, Sarah gave birth to Isaac. After Isaac was born another conflict developed in the house of Abraham. Hagar and Ishmael were caught teasing Isaac. This made Sarah very upset. She went to Abraham and requested that he send Hagar and Ishmael away, and he did.

The Bible states in Genesis 21:11, that Abraham was upset at the thought of sending Ishmael away. Abraham loved Ishmael but Sarah would not tolerate him teasing Isaac or sharing the inheritance with Isaac. When Abraham sent Hagar and Ishmael away, he did not send enough food and water to sustain them. Ishmael was at the point of death from lack of food and water. Hagar could not bear to see her son die so she laid him under a tree, walked away and cried. God heard Ishmael crying and he spoke to Hagar. God showed Hagar a fountain of water in the desert and reassured her of his promises that He had made to her.

Throughout the lives of these two women, they both made some very poor decisions. They both had shortcomings and character flaws. Hagar, Sarah and Abraham were all were hurt by their decisions. Sarah and Hagar did not have the best relationship with each other due to lack of respect for each other fueled by pride. The only thing they had in common was a man named Abraham who was the father of their children. God still worked everything out for their good and His glory.

Application, Thoughts & Questions

Application

Married couples need to be mindful of the decisions made within the marriage. Internal problems that arise within the marriage need to be resolved between the spouses and God. In Mark 10:9 *it states: therefore what God has joined together let no one separate.* The word "man" in that verse, not only refers to outsiders, but it also refers to the husband or wife in the marriage. Abraham and Sarah's marriage had some dysfunction within, but God was still able to make things work out for *their* and *our* good.

Thought

Genesis 15:6 states, Abraham believed the Lord and he credited it to him as righteousness. Being a Christian does not mean that you will always make good decisions. But it is our belief in God that makes us righteous. God blessed Abraham and his family despite their dysfunction, and the same God will bless you and your family as well if you keep trusting, following and believing in His word.

Questions

1. If you are married, identify if there is any dysfunction within your marriage, family, or other relationships. What changes would you like to occur within the dysfunction according to the Word of God?

_____

_____

_____

_____

_____

2. Have you ever used your influence to manipulate someone else for your own personal gain? How did that manipulation affect your relationship with that person? Or, have you been manipulated to do things because of someone else. Did you end up getting hurt because of it?

_____

_____

_____

_____

_____

_____

3. Hagar realized that God saw her in her misery and unfortunate circumstance, but he assured her that everything was going to be okay. Like Hagar, we have to acknowledge that God sees us, and He will work things out for our favor if we just believe in Him and do what He says. If you are that woman who has been mistreated, abused, abandoned or have made poor decisions, are you willing to let God "see you"? Are you ready to surrender to Him?

_____

_____

_____

_____

_____

_____

4. Custody battles, child support orders, divorce decrees, paternity test and other factors can arouse with dealing with relationships gone bad with children. Unfortunately, the end result is that the children often suffer the most. Do you know some people who are in this type of situation? What are some problems that you notice, if any, within the family?

_____

_____

_____

_____

_____

_____

_____

5. Just like Hagar, we all have the potential of being prideful. A believer who walks in pride will soon find herself out of God's will because pride blinds the truth. Exalting yourself above your master, fueled by pride, will lead to expulsion from a blessed place. What blessings have you missed by being prideful?

_____

_____

_____

_____

_____

_____

_____

6. If you put God first He will lead and guide you. Putting God first means you have to put Him before your feelings, emotions, situation and circumstances. When God speaks, He usually gives you specific instruction on how to handle yourself. Do not forget the words He speaks to you as they can keep you from a lot of unnecessary hurt, pain and poor decisions. What painful things have God spoken to you about? Reflect on the word He gave when you face future challenges.

_____
_____
_____
_____
_____
_____
_____

Chapter 2
Rebeckah

Rebeckah's act of intercession was to go to the Lord and inquire about her unborn sons. As a result of her asking, a prophetic word was spoken to the future generations of Israel and the world.

Rebekah

Isaac prayed to the Lord on behalf of his wife, because she was childless. The Lord answered his prayer, and his wife Rebekah became pregnant. The babies jostled each other within her, and she said, "Why is this happening to me?" So she went to inquire of the Lord.

The Lord said to her, "Two nations are in your womb, and two peoples from within you will be separated; one people will be stronger than the other, and the older will serve the younger."

When the time came for her to give birth, there were twin boys in her womb. The first to come out was red, and his whole body was like a hairy garment; so they named him Esau. After this, his brother came out, with his hand grasping Esau's heel; so he was named Jacob. Isaac was sixty years old when Rebekah gave birth to them (Gen. 25:21-26).

Rebekah was a vessel God chose to birth two sons. Their descendants would become mighty nations. Isaac knew God and what He could do. He prayed to Him when Rebekah was unable to have children. God answered his prayer. During her pregnancy there was a physical and spiritual struggle going on in her womb between her unborn babies. She asked God "what is happening to me?" And God answered.

It was the manifestation of the birth of two nations in the spirit. The struggle inside of her was the foreshadowing of how the two nations would physically struggle amongst each other for "birthrights" for centuries to come.

We have all at some point in our life asked God, "What is

happening to me?" when we're going through things that we totally did not understand. Rebekah however, directly asked the question to God, the only one who was able answer her. This is a good lesson because we will go through troubling times in our lives. We often go to our friends and families for advice, rather than inquiring an answer from God. As seen in the passage of scripture, God answered her.

What comes to my mind when I read this part of scripture is that, maybe God allowed her to be baron for a while because He knew what was going to happen before it actually happened. He knew that Rebekah was going to have a complicated pregnancy. When He did answer Rebekah, he came to her with a spiritual word, not a physical one. What was going on inside of her had nothing to do with something being wrong with her pregnancy; it had to do with the destinies of her two sons.

The next time you are having one of those "what is going on with me" moments, take time to remember that it may not necessarily be about you. It could just be that something is manifesting in the spiritual realm that is making its way to the earth through you–a vessel that God has chosen. This may be a difficult question to understand, but we all go through times in our lives when we do not understand why so many things are happening. Yet, we must remember that God did not send us to earth without a purpose.

If you are pregnant (or one day desire to become a mother) start now praying for your unborn child. We all have destinies to fulfill in life and mothers have a responsibility to raise children in a way that will help them to fulfill the calling on their life.

Acts of Intercession

Lastly, what we can learn about Rebekah's story is that it is not always about *us*. Many times we go through hard times in our life for somebody else. Rebekah's difficult pregnancy was a testimony to the future generations. She was unable to have children, but because God heard her husband's prayer she bore children. She had a difficult pregnancy, but she ended up giving birth to two nations. One of her seeds would be in the direct lineage of Christ.

That testimony alone should bring hope to someone who is barren. You do not have to be seeking a child to be barren, but maybe your life has taken you to a place of emptiness. Emptiness in your career, marriage, emotions, dreams, and family; yet learn from Rebekah's story.

Inquire to God about your situation and expect an answer. He may not answer the way you think He should, but His answer will be an individual one for your situation.

Application, Thoughts & Questions

Application
Rebekah was unable to have children until the appointed time of conception. Her husband prayed for her and God answered. Rebekah's husband had a relationship with God and knew God for himself. It is always great to have a husband that will intercede for his wife.

Thought
If the husband can demonstrate a prayer life that gets results, it will be easy for the wife to follow the same path through trusting and believing that God will hear and answer prayer.

Questions
1. Who has been an example/inspiration in your life as it relates to prayer?

_____
_____
_____
_____
_____
_____
_____

2. Have you ever questioned God about what is going on with you? What was his response?

_____
_____
_____
_____
_____
_____
_____

3. Rebekah was a vessel that was chosen by God to birth two nations. What is God birthing in you?

_____
_____
_____
_____
_____
_____
_____

If you have a children write out a prayer for them.

_____
_____
_____
_____
_____
_____
_____

Write your testimony on how God has answered your prayer request.

_____
_____
_____
_____
_____
_____
_____

Chapter 3

Rachel and Leah

**Rachel and Leah's act of intercession
was birthing the nation of Israel.**

Rachel & Leah

When the Lord saw that Leah was not loved, he enabled her to conceive, but Rachel remained childless. Leah became pregnant and gave birth to a son. She named him Reuben, for she said, "It is because the Lord has seen my misery. Surely my husband will love me now."

She conceived again, and when she gave birth to a son she said, "Because the Lord heard that I am not loved, he gave me this one too." So she named him Simeon.

Again she conceived, and when she gave birth to a son she said, "Now at last my husband will become attached to me, because I have borne him three sons." So he was named Levi.

She conceived again, and when she gave birth to a son she said, "This time I will praise the Lord." So she named him Judah. Then she stopped having children. (Gen. 29:31-35).

When Rachel saw that she was not bearing Jacob any children, she became jealous of her sister. So she said to Jacob, "Give me children, or I'll die!"

Jacob became angry with her and said, "Am I in the place of God, who has kept you from having children?"

Then she said, "Here is Bilhah, my servant. Sleep with her so that she can bear children for me and I too can build a family through her."

So she gave him her servant Bilhah as a wife. Jacob slept with her, and she became pregnant and bore him a son. Then Rachel said,

"God has vindicated me; he has listened to my plea and given me a son." Because of this she named him Dan.

Rachel's servant Bilhah conceived again and bore Jacob a second son. Then Rachel said, "I have had a great struggle with my sister, and I have won." So she named him Naphtali.

When Leah saw that she had stopped having children, she took her servant Zilpah and gave her to Jacob as a wife. Leah's servant Zilpah bore Jacob a son. Then Leah said, "What good fortune!" So she named him Gad.

Leah's servant Zilpah bore Jacob a second son. Then Leah said, "How happy I am! The women will call me happy." So she named him Asher.

During wheat harvest, Reuben went out into the fields and found some mandrake plants, which he brought to his mother Leah. Rachel said to Leah, "Please give me some of your son's mandrakes."

But she said to her, "Wasn't it enough that you took away my husband? Will you take my son's mandrakes too?"

"Very well," Rachel said, "he can sleep with you tonight in return for your son's mandrakes."

So when Jacob came in from the fields that evening, Leah went out to meet him. "You must sleep with me," she said. "I have hired you with my son's mandrakes." So he slept with her that night.

God listened to Leah, and she became pregnant and bore Jacob a fifth son. Then Leah said, "God has rewarded me for giving my servant to my husband." So she named him Issachar.

Leah conceived again and bore Jacob a sixth son. Then Leah said,

"God has presented me with a precious gift. This time my husband will treat me with honor, because I have borne him six sons." So she named him Zebulun.

Sometime later she gave birth to a daughter and named her Dinah.

Then God remembered Rachel; he listened to her and enabled her to conceive (Gen. 30:1-22).

This is an extreme case of sibling rivalry. Jacob wanted to marry Rachel because she was more physically attractive than Leah. But their dad tricked Jacob into marrying Leah first. He wouldn't be allowed to marry Rachel for seven more years. (Eventually, Jacob fled from his father-in-law because of his constant unfair treatment.)

In the meantime, it must have been hard for Leah to be married to a man who did not want to be with her. In biblical times, it was common for men to have multiple wives, even though it was not God's original plan. Today, polygamy is outlawed. However, we see many couples that are in "triangle" relationships.

In most cases it is two women in a relationship with one man (but there can be other combinations of this as well). The man is not willing to commit to just one woman; he wants to have both of them at the same time. In these types of relationships, someone does not have their needs met. Children conceived through these relationships also may suffer because the man is dividing his time between women.

When a man (or a woman) is "playing around" and refuses to commit to monogamy, it creates disastrous results. Many women (or men) accept this type of relationship for various reasons. Low self-esteem, personal views about love or marriage, soul-ties, abuse, are some examples why people stay in such relationships.

God created one man and one woman in the Garden of Eden and they were husband and wife. God did not create multiple husbands and wives to be married together as He knew how dysfunctional it could become. In Jacob's case, God was able to make dysfunction function for His glory. God had made a promise to Abraham and His promise had to be fulfilled through Jacob.

Leah felt so unloved by Jacob and this reflected in the naming of her first three children, yet by the time she birthed her fourth child, her heart had changed. She took her focus off Jacob and put it on God. She named her child Judah which means this time I will praise the Lord. She was looking for love from Jacob and he did not provide that for her, but God loved her.

Leah realized, through Judah, that she needed to direct her attention to God and come out of her misery of rejection. Man may reject you but God will never leave or forsake you. God's love comes without conditions.

Jacob's love for Rachel was conditional because of her physical appearance. God's unconditional love reflects his affection for the person he created, and everything that God creates is good. Many people stay in a "love triangle" because they are longing for someone to love them. They lower their standards and share a person with someone else rather than wait for God and experience His total unconditional love and everything that He has for them.

Acts of Intercession

Rachel and Leah were two determined sisters on a mission for Jacob's attention. Both sisters were competing for what we all desire–love and affection. The competition between them consisted of who could give Jacob the most sons. Leah was the first to bear the four children of Jacob. This made Rachel jealous because she was unable to have children at the time.

So, Rachel got her servants involved to bear children for her. In turn, Leah did the same thing with her servants. Eleven children in total were produce through their rivalry over Jacob. Twelve tribes of Israel would be represented through their sons (Joseph had two sons who took his place within the nation).

Little did they know that this was more than just a competition, they were being used to birth a nation. The names of their children had meaning. The meaning of their names would manifest through the generations to come. The competition between the sisters would also manifest through the children and their offspring as well (Joseph and his brothers, Israel dividing into two kingdoms are some examples).

Rachel and Leah were two chosen imperfect vessels used by God to bring forth Jacob's children and the nation of Israel. You may have experienced a triangle relationship in your life, but just like we have learned, God can still use you. A great and mighty nation came through the triangle of Leah, Rachel, and Jacob.

Application, Thoughts & Questions

Questions

1. Do you have siblings who you don't always see "eye to eye" with? Have you ever felt competition between the two of you?

_____
_____
_____
_____
_____
_____
_____

2. Have you ever loved someone who you felt did not love you back? How did it make you feel?

_____
_____
_____
_____
_____

3. There were two obvious problems going on with Leah and Rachel. Jacob did not love Leah but she was able to bore him children. Rachel became jealous of Leah because she could not have children when Leah was conceiving.

Rejection and jealousy was fueling the rift between Rachel and Leah. The common denominator between them was a man named Jacob. Can you relate to their problem? Give examples.

_____
_____
_____

4. If you are a woman who is currently in this type of relationship, these questions are for you to think about:

Do you want to live the rest of your life like this?

Why do you feel you are not worthy of faithfulness?

What has God told you about this relationship?

Are you even hearing from God at all?

What brought you to this point in your life?

_____
_____
_____
_____
_____
_____
_____

5. Do you want to change the direction that your life is going? If yes, then pray for a "Judah" experience. Let your praise be so focused on God that things will begin to change in your life. Leah's problem was not Jacob or Rachel.

Her problem was internalizing the pain of rejection. What are some things you are internalizing? Write them out and pray for God to heal you in those areas.

Chapter 4

Tamar

The intercessional act of Tamar was in the form of this question: What would happen if Tamar did not conceive with Judah? The fact is, she did, and her offspring were a part of Christ lineage.

 Tamar

Judah got a wife for Er, his firstborn, and her name was Tamar. But Er, Judah's first born, was wicked in the Lord's sight; so the Lord put him to death.

Then Judah said to Onan, "Sleep with your brother's wife and fulfill your duty to her as a brother-in-law to raise up offspring for your brother." But Onan knew that the child would not be his; so whenever he slept with his brother's wife, he spilled his semen on the ground to keep from providing offspring for his brother. What he did was wicked in the Lord's sight; so the Lord put him to death also.

Judah then said to his daughter-in-law Tamar, "Live as a widow in your father's household until my son Shelah grows up." For he thought, "He may die too, just like his brothers." So Tamar went to live in her father's household.

After a long time Judah's wife, the daughter of Shua, died. When Judah had recovered from his grief, he went up to Timnah, to the men who were shearing his sheep, and his friend Hirah the Adullamite went with him.

When Tamar was told, "Your father-in-law is on his way to Timnah to shear his sheep," she took off her widow's clothes, covered herself with a veil to disguise herself, and then sat down at the entrance to Enaim, which is on the road to Timnah. For she saw that, though Shelah had now grown up, she had not been given to him as his wife.

Shana Wise

When Judah saw her, he thought she was a prostitute, for she had covered her face. Not realizing that she was his daughter-in-law, he went over to her by the roadside and said, "Come now, let me sleep with you."

"And what will you give me to sleep with you?" she asked.

"I'll send you a young goat from my flock," he said.

"Will you give me something as a pledge until you send it?" she asked.

He said, "What pledge should I give you?"

"Your seal and its cord, and the staff in your hand," she answered. So he gave them to her and slept with her, and she became pregnant by him. After she left, she took off her veil and put on her widow's clothes again.

Meanwhile Judah sent the young goat by his friend the Adullamite in order to get his pledge back from the woman, but he did not find her. He asked the men who lived there, "Where is the shrine prostitute who was beside the road at Enaim?"

"There hasn't been any shrine prostitute here," they said.

So he went back to Judah and said, "I didn't find her. Besides, the men who lived there said, 'There hasn't been any shrine prostitute here.'"

Then Judah said, "Let her keep what she has, or we will become a laughingstock. After all, I did send her this young goat, but you didn't find her."

Acts of Intercession

About three months later Judah was told, "Your daughter-in-law Tamar is guilty of prostitution, and as a result she is now pregnant."

Judah said, "Bring her out and have her burned to death!"

As she was being brought out, she sent a message to her father-in-law. "I am pregnant by the man who owns these," she said. And she added, "See if you recognize whose seal and cord and staff these are."

Judah recognized them and said, "She is more righteous than I, since I wouldn't give her to my son Shelah." And he did not sleep with her again.

When the time came for her to give birth, there were twin boys in her womb. As she was giving birth, one of them put out his hand; so the midwife took a scarlet thread and tied it on his wrist and said, "This one came out first." But when he drew back his hand, his brother came out, and she said, "So this is how you have broken out!" And he was named Perez. Then his brother, who had the scarlet thread on his wrist, came out. And he was named Zerah (Gen. 38:6-30).

This passage of the Bible is full of scandal and deceit. It reminds me of the Maury Show where different women appear on the show to discover who the father of their child is through DNA testing. Before the results, the mother and father of the child have a chance to tell their side of the story in regards to their relationship, or lack thereof.

Many times the father denies that the child is his and the mother swears that he is the father. It is during this point of the show that it gets pretty comical. Emotions are flying and tensions are escalating, all while their dysfunctional situation is displayed in front of a live television audience to millions around the world.

When the results come in, the host Maury Povich, announces that either the man is or is not the child's father. That's when the show really gets good! All kinds of emotions arise between the mother and the father depending on the results. People leave happy, hurt, deceived, angry, mournful, or boastful.

The whole time, I am watching the show like, "this is a hot ghetto mess!" But, the scripture that comes to mind as I watch this show is, Romans 5:20(b), But where sin abounded, grace did much more abound.

Tamar was a woman who shows us that God can still work out things in our favor, even if we do not always make good decisions. This text involves the family of Judah and the main characters include Judah, his sons, and Tamar his daughter in-law. To summarize this story, Tamar was first married to Judah's firstborn son named Er and he was wicked in God's eyes so God killed him. Er died before Tamar conceived any children.

As custom would have it, Tamar was to marry the next eldest son named Onan. When Onan and Tamar had sex, Onan withdrew himself from her so she would not get pregnant. His motive had to do with birthrights of the unborn child. In their culture, the next eldest brother was to take the widow of his brother, and if they had any children together that child would still be considered the deceased heir.

Since Er was the firstborn son of Judah, Er's son would

be first to Judah inheritance. When Onan did this act with Tamar, it angered God so much that He killed him as well.

Next in line of marrying Tamar was Judah's youngest son Shelah, but at the time Shelah was still a child. So Judah told Tamar, go home to your father's house as a widow, and wait until my youngest son is grown and I will give you to marry him. So she did as she was told.

Meanwhile Judah's wife died. During Judah's period of mourning, he went away to visit his friend and help them tend to the sheep. Tamar lived nearby where Judah was visiting and she heard that he was coming to town. During this time, she found out that Judah's youngest son Shelah had grown up, and that Judah reneged on his promise to her.

Once again, the wrong motives of Judah stepped in the way of doing the right thing. He looked upon Tamar as being bad luck to his family. Both of his sons died after they married Tamar, and he figured that he would save his youngest son by not letting him marry her.

The truth of his sons' death was not because of Tamar, but because they were wicked and evil in the sight of the Lord. Tamar started taking control of her situation. She devised a plan to conceive a child within Judah's bloodline. Tamar was done with (messing around) with Judah's sons; she was going to the head of the house, Judah!

Women in biblical days did not have many rights. They were viewed as property. They were worth a little bit more than a dog. They surely did not have any say within their marriages or family. Whatever was going on within their marriage they just had to deal with it.

In this case, once Tamar married Ur, she became a part of Judah's family. So, when a brother died she was just passed down to the next. I am sure Tamar did not have a problem with the customs of those days, but I am sure she did not like the way she was treated–or mistreated within the family. She probably felt humiliated, lonely, and desperate, victimized, and of low self esteem.

The person who was suppose do the right thing was Judah. Yet, when it was time for him to give Shelah to be her husband he backed down for his own selfish reasons. Judah probably thought that he would just "put Tamar away." He shunned her by viewing her as a curse to his family.

Now, let us not forget that this was not the first time in Judah's life that he carried a "dirty little secret." He was one of the brothers who sold Joseph into slavery and went back and told his father Jacob that Joseph was dead. So Judah already had issues with doing the right thing when it came to family.

Tamar thought in her mind that desperate times called for desperate measures. She may have been at the lowest point in her life. She was widowed twice. She was living back home with her father (in which, if he had any sons, she would not have rights to his inheritance). She was childless. She was "put away" by Judah's family. She was the forgotten one. Her future did not look good at all.

She wanted a child. Not only did she want a child, she wanted her child to be born in the bloodline of Judah. She knew that even though Judah's family was very dysfunctional, they were still a blessed people. Not because of who they were, but because of the God they served.

Tamar went and posed as a prostitute along the roadside where her father-in-law, Judah was passing through. Judah, grieving from the death of his wife, notices her not as Tamar, but as a hooker. And he slept with her. Tamar knew exactly what she was doing and who she was doing it with. Judah promised to pay Tamar with a calf, but for collateral Tamar took his personal staff, a ribbon, and bracelets. When Judah went back to pay Tamar she was nowhere to be found. Judah went home, and that was that.

Some months after the night of deception, Tamar was pregnant and word got back to Judah. Judah was ready to punish Tamar by death for getting pregnant out of wedlock. When Tamar was brought to him, she gave him the collateral he left with her (who he thought was a prostitute). Judah could not deny that the baby was his.

He could not deny that he sinned against Tamar and against God for sleeping with the one who he thought was a strange prostitute AND for not giving his son Shelah, to marry her. Judah admitted his sin and even stated that Tamar was more righteous than he. He vowed never to sleep with Tamar again.

We still live in a society where a woman who "sleeps around" is looked down upon, while a man (Judah, for example) who does the same, is not treated with the same regard. You may currently be–or have in the past, slept around with different men. You may also have sold your body for money, drugs or material things. All of us have different reasons and motives why we do things. Tamar's' motive may have been revenge, desperation, low self-esteem, or hopelessness. But her motives and actions did not stop God's plan for her life.

Tamar may have felt trapped in her current situation (childless, widowed, mistreated, and put away). She resorted to posing (acting) as a prostitute (unto her father-in-law Judah). Tamar was risking her health, reputation, living situation (at her father's house), and her life; all in the hopes of conceiving a child. Just like Tamar, we also can make poor decisions out of despair. Sometimes we keep making the same mistakes over and over again because of the way we view our self or past or current situation.

If you are that woman or man, please know that God specializes in despair. You do not have to keep living a life full of poor decisions and past hurts. You can change with God's help. It is important that we learn how to forgive those who have mistreated us. Judah and his sons mistreated Tamar, but God still worked everything out in Tamar's favor.

Judah ended up repenting for his wrong doings. (Remember that God will take care of those who mistreat you in His own way, not ours.) Tamar's ultimate motive and desire was to birth a child within Judah's family. God knew what she wanted and granted it unto her (regardless of the way she went about conceiving).

Today is a new day and God is able to do a new thing in your life! Just like Tamar, you can overcome your bad situation. God will work out your past, present and future for your good and for His glory. Your past cannot stop your destiny. If you are feeling guilt from your current or past mistakes, just know that it does not stop God's unfailing love for you or the plans that he has for your life. Regardless if someone else has mistreated or misused you, their actions do not define who you are.

Tamar had twins that would be offspring in the lineage of Christ despite the dysfunction within Judah's family! In the end Romans 8:28 still prevailed. Why? God can take a dysfunctional family and make it function for His glory.

Application, Thoughts & Questions

Application

You may be a woman who feels that you have (gotten) the short end of the stick in life. You may have some of the same feelings Tamar had as it relates to men doing you wrong, but look into your life to see how God is working behind the scenes in our lives.

Thought

As I was researching this text, I stumbled across a commentary where the author deemed Tamar as being a low-life woman. He portrayed her as an evil whore who happened to be a part of Judah's family. I figured this particular author was bias regarding God's word.

We, as believers, must be able to interpret the scriptures through a level of grace. Jesus Christ came to fulfill the law, meaning there is no more condemnation to those that are in Christ Jesus. As I studied this story, I was able to see God's plan working out for his chosen people.

Questions

1. Have you experienced being mistreated by a man or woman in your life? Write down your feelings as it relates to them and their treatment of you.

_____
_____
_____
_____
_____
_____
_____
_____
_____
_____
_____

2. If any, write out past situations that you have not completely healed from. Then write what God is telling you as it relates to this passage of scripture.

_____
_____
_____
_____
_____
_____
_____

3. What are your dreams and desires? (List them out below).

_____
_____
_____
_____
_____
_____

4. What do you want God to change about you?

_____
_____
_____
_____

If you have not forgiven those who have mistreated you, do it today. Forgiveness is more beneficial for you than the other person. God blessed Tamar with TWO children. God blesses those who forgive. If you are having a hard time forgiving, allow the Lord to come into your heart and show you how to forgive, through His son Jesus Christ.

Write out your thoughts as it relates to forgiveness.

_____
_____
_____
_____
_____

_____
_____
_____
_____
_____

_____
_____
_____
_____
_____

_____
_____
_____
_____
_____

_____
_____
_____
_____
_____

Chapter 5
Shiphrah & Puah

The midwives, Shiphrah and Puah, act of intercession was not to kill the Hebrew newborn boys as ordered.

Shiphrah & Puah

The king of Egypt said to the Hebrew midwives, whose names were Shiphrah and Puah, "When you are helping the Hebrew women during childbirth on the delivery stool, if you see that the baby is a boy, kill him; but if it is a girl, let her live."

The midwives, however, feared God and did not do what the king of Egypt had told them to do; they let the boys live. Then the king of Egypt summoned the midwives and asked them, "Why have you done this? Why have you let the boys live?"

The midwives answered Pharaoh, "Hebrew women are not like Egyptian women; they are vigorous and give birth before the midwives arrive."
So God was kind to the midwives and the people increased and became even more numerous. And because the midwives feared God, he gave them families of their own (Ex. 1:15-21).

Here is a story of two women who worshipped and honored the true and living God. Their reverence for God spilled from their personal lives to their professional lives. The King of Egypt asked them to do something that compromised their moral values and their worship toward God.

He ordered them to kill all male babies of Hebraic ethnicity during their delivery. Could you imagine physically killing a newborn baby, knowing that it is not your will, but for someone else's evil will?

Shiphrah and Puah were professionally known as midwives

in the community of Egypt. Everybody in the Egyptian and Hebraic community used these ladies' services when it was time for a woman to give birth. These ladies were not just lip-service believers who only worshipped God when it was convenient for them. They were obedient to the faith, even when it meant that it would cause them their job or their life. They feared God more than Pharaoh. Therefore, they did not kill any baby boys.

The enemy was using Pharaoh to execute his plan of death for the nation of Israelites; but God used two midwives to assist in bringing forth life of the nation. Remember that your acts of obedience today can affect the nation of tomorrow.

The midwives knew that they belonged to God, and most importantly that these children belonged to Him as well. They knew that God does not make mistakes when it comes to human life. And despite the order from Pharaoh to kill newborn male babies, they refused. They were willing to sacrifice their life so that someone else could live.

Application, Thoughts & Questions

Thoughts

You may be a woman who has contact with the community you live in as it relates to your job, profession, or trade. Do you view your job as just work or can you see your kingdom connection to your assigned duties?

Reflect on how this passage of scripture relates to you and your purpose.

Question

1. There are times in our everyday lives when people may try to manipulate us to compromise our personal beliefs and values, just as the Pharaoh did the midwives. It may happen in our homes, on our jobs, with friends or family.

Are you willing to stand up for what you believe? If you knew what you believed could cause you to lose friends, relationships, jobs, reputations, and even your life would you take the risk to please God? If not, what are the things that are holding you back from standing up for yourself and your God?

_____
_____
_____
_____
_____
_____
_____

Chapter 6
Miriam &
Pharaoh's Daughter

Miriam's act of intercession was to follow her
brother and advocate for his wellbeing.
Pharaoh's daughter act of intercession
was raising Moses as her own child.

Miriam & Pharaoh's Daughter

Now a man of the tribe of Levi married a Levite woman, and she became pregnant and gave birth to a son. When she saw that he was a fine child, she hid him for three months. But when she could hide him no longer, she got a papyrus basket for him and coated it with tar and pitch. Then she placed the child in it and put it among the reeds along the bank of the Nile. His sister stood at a distance to see what would happen to him.

Then Pharaoh's daughter went down to the Nile to bathe, and her attendants were walking along the riverbank. She saw the basket among the reeds and sent her female slave to get it. She opened it and saw the baby. He was crying, and she felt sorry for him. "This is one of the Hebrew babies," she said.

Then his sister asked Pharaoh's daughter, "Shall I go and get one of the Hebrew women to nurse the baby for you?"
"Yes, go," she answered. So the girl went and got the baby's mother. Pharaoh's daughter said to her, "Take this baby and nurse him for me, and I will pay you."

So the woman took the baby and nursed him. When the child grew older, she took him to Pharaoh's daughter and he became her son. She named him Moses, saying, "I drew him out of the water" (Ex. 2:1-10).

During this time in Egypt, Pharaoh ordered that all Hebrew boys under the age of two be executed. Moses and Miriam's parents found Moses to be a special and anointed baby boy. So they hid him at home.

When they could no longer hide him, they sent him down the river in a basket. Death was a constant threat for Moses (between Pharaohs' orders and the elements of the Nile River). Yet, of all the members of the family, it was Miriam who followed her baby brother, down the river, until he made it to his final divine destination, which was Pharaohs' daughter.

Miriam waited for the opportune time to speak and advocate for her brother. She saw the heart of Pharaohs' daughter as she had compassion for Moses. In other words, she bonded with him instantly.

In my own life, I observed my brother living a life that did not "meet my expectations." During his teenage and early adult life, I felt that he wasn't saved because of the way he chose to live his life. I was the type of Christian who knew Christ and wanted to "Bible thump" every time my brother came around. I would tell him, "You need to get saved." Or, "God is not pleased with your lifestyle."

It came to the point, that my brother did not want to come around or talk to me about anything because I was always, "preaching to him". He felt that I was judging his lifestyle and condemning him. So, one day I prayed for my brother and asked the Lord to save and protect him. The Lord spoke to me and said that He needed me to take up my "Miriam position" in my brother's life. Just like Miriam, I had to watch my brother from a distance go down the "river of life."

God reminded me that Moses had to travel down his own road. He was put into dangerous situations (Nile River), but God's purpose for Moses prevails, and if He did it for Moses, He would do the same thing for my brother. He also told me that I was turning my brother off Christ because I came with a condemning word instead of a word of unconditional love and compassion.

Since the day, whenever my brother comes around I make sure not to judge him or give him a condemning word. I had to start my conversations in "the place where he was." I had to make sure first and foremost that I loved him uncondi-tionally and that I had his back no matter what. Now that does not mean that I compromised my Christian values, but I learned how to discern my witnessing of Christ and my communication skills with the word.

Miriam did not speak to Pharaoh's daughter until the appro-priate time. I had to learn *when* to talk to my brother. Now, my brother feels comfortable talking with me about God and spiritual topics. Pharaohs' daughter also played an impor-tant part in Moses' success. All of us in life have some kind of role to play, whether as an employee, daughter, mother, sister, friend, or whatever. We all are connected to somebody.

Being Pharaoh's daughter came with certain responsibilities. She was a representation of the law of the land. In Mosses' situation, she could have followed her father's decree and gave Moses up to be killed. Yet, she had love and compassion for this baby and went against her father's evil morals and values to do the right thing. Not only did she spare Moses' life, she raised him as one of her own. She raised a child who was not of her ethnicity, faith, or bloodline; yet because of her love and compassion towards Moses, she saved his life.

There will be times in our life where we are going to have to "go against the grain". In our society and culture we are going to confront issues that deal with life and death such as the death penalty, abortions, murder and genocide. These issues arise in elections, educational intuitions, and various other political, business and organizational arenas.

Our decisions today will affect strangers tomorrow. Moses was the one chosen to deliver a nation out of slavery. God spared his life through Pharaohs' daughter. Not only did God spare his life, Moses grew up in the palace and eventually was instrumental in delivering the Israelites out of Egypt.

Application, Thoughts & Questions

Thoughts

I love this story in the Bible because Miriam shows us how to "watch from a distance". Miriam's story helped me in my personal life in regards to my baby brother. He and I are twelve years apart. I had accepted Jesus Christ as my Lord and savior when I was 20 years old. As I grew in Christ, I watched my brother grow up physically and spiritually as well.

When we help someone through our actions of love and compassion, we do not know how it is going to impact them and the ones that they are connected to. Many times we will have to stand up for what is moral and righteous even if it means it will cost us something. The cost may be your reputation, losing friends, work, or just being unpopular, or even your life, but are you willing to take that risk so that someone else may live? Have you?

Question

1. I needed to take a "Miriam Position" with my brother, which is to watch (and pray) from a distance. Who has God placed in your life that you need to take a "Miriam position on"? How will you respond differently?

_____
_____
_____
_____
_____
_____
_____

Chapter 7
Zipporah

Zipporah's act of intercession was doing the right thing for her family, even though she didn't agree with it.

Zipporah

At a lodging place on the way, the Lord met Moses and was about to kill him. But Zipporah took a flint knife, cut off her son's foreskin and touched Moses' feet with it. "Surely you are a bridegroom of blood to me," she said. So the Lord let him alone. (At that time she said "bridegroom of blood," referring to circumcision.) (Ex. 4:24-26).

This is one of many interesting stories in the Bible. Moses received his calling from God in the wilderness. He was instructed to return to Egypt and deliver his people from slavery. He had married Zipporah—a girl not of his background and had a son. As Moses and his family were traveling back to Egypt God gave him instructions to circumcise his son.

Zipporah did not want her baby boy to be subject to physical pain inflicted by her husband. This act of circumcision was not a norm in her cultural background. She protested the circumcision and Moses gave in to her request. However, when Moses refused God's request, God sought to kill him.

A frightened Zipporah took action and did the very thing she urged Moses not to do. She circumcise her son and threw the foreskin on Moses so that he would live. Zipporah circumcised her son with an attitude, based on the comment she made when she threw the foreskin on Moses. She, like us, may have to do the right thing even when we do not want to. It is also important that we obey God wholeheartedly. God does not ask us to do things that will harm us or our families. All of His commandments are for our good even if we do not understand it or it does not "feel good to us".

Zipporah may have heard that her husband had a calling on his life. But, up until God moved to kill Moses, she didn't realize how this "calling" was going to affect her and her children, and the history of Israel. We as women must learn how to use our influence wisely with our husbands. We have to recognize if our will (feelings and emotions) goes against God's original plan and purpose for our husbands.

We live in a society where women are made to feel as if she does not need a man to support her, or help raise her kids, or tell her what to do. Many of us have been raised to be inde-pendent of the need for a man. Yet, we must remember the God we serve. He does not make mistakes. He created male and female. He instituted marriage in the Garden of Eden. Once we have children we must remember that the child has two parents, not just one.

Zipporah did not want Moses to deal with their son in re-gards to circumcising him. There are times when we must remember that it takes a man to raise a boy. No disrespect to single mothers, because many times a single mother has to raise a man child all by herself, and there is nothing wrong with that if the child's father is not around. In this case, how-ever, Moses was present in the home. His wife decided to overstep her boundaries and interfere with Moses assign-ment.

As you examine your own marriage, are there any areas that you find yourself overstepping your boundaries with your husband? For example, when your husband tells your kids to do something that you do not like (something that will not mentally or physically hurt then), do you tell your kids something different?

Moses' calling was directly related to deliverance of a nation out of Egypt. Before he arrived back to Egypt, there had to be a spiritual and physical circumcision done on all the males in the household. Circumcision is a symbol for God's children, to be separated unto Himself, for His special purpose. It was at this moment that God was going to do something special in the earth's realm. History was about to change, and Moses was going to be instrumental in bringing it to pass.

We must remember that marriage is an equal partnership, in where both parties are needed to make it work. It is great if you are able to confess that you may have a problem with control because we serve a God who can change us. Zipporah was able to implement that very thing she detested, Moses lived, and his purpose was fulfilled.

Application, Thoughts & Questions

Application

When we marry the man that God has designed for us, he is going to do something great in that man's life. God is always doing a new thing in our lives. So, when he gives your husband a vision, there are going to be times where you do not understand it, or may flat out disagree with it. Yet, you still must trust the God in him.

Do not be like Zipporah and cause your man to stumble in the mist of God's plan. As you see, it almost meant death unto Moses. Worst of all, if Moses would have died; it would have delayed the Israelites getting out of bondage.

Thought

Isn't it funny how wives can lead their husbands into disobedience? When God gives our husbands something to do, we must trust the God in them, even if it means putting our personal feelings to the side.

Questions

1. Have you ever lead your husband or someone else in disobedience because you didn't agree with them or understand what God was doing in their life? What was the outcome?

_____
_____
_____
_____
_____
_____
_____
_____

2. Are you aware of your connection to the vision that God has given your husband? Are you on one accord with him? How do you know that you are on one accord with him?

_____

_____

_____

_____

_____

3. If he does not have a vision, do you trust that God will give him one for your family? Write out a prayer for your husband, your marriage, your children, and your purpose for the family unit.

_____

_____

_____

_____

_____

4. If you are not on one accord, what is your desire for your marriage? Are you willing to sacrifice your feelings and emotions to make it work if he is willing?

_____

_____

_____

_____

_____

_____

5. Do you see how disobedience can affect someone else's deliverance?

_____
_____
_____
_____
_____
_____

6. Are you on one accord with disciplining the kids, finances, communication, in-laws and other family members—baby mama/daddy—and various other issues that involve marriage?

_____
_____
_____
_____
_____
_____

7. Lastly, do you find yourself dominating the marriage and/or finding yourself needing to be in control of the house, kids, and your husband? Do you want to change but don't know how? Confess your fault to God, obey what He tells you to do, and watch Him change your life and marriage.

_____
_____
_____
_____
_____

Chapter 8

The Daughters of Zelophehad

Their act of intercession was pleading their case (of inheritance), in their father's name, not for only their family's sake, but for future women who would be placed in the same situation as them.

Shana Wise

The Daughters of Zelophehad

The daughters of Zelophehad son of Hepher, the son of Gilead, the son of Makir, the son of Manasseh, belonged to the clans of Manasseh son of Joseph. The names of the daughters were Mahlah, Noah, Hoglah, Milkah and Tirzah. They came forward and stood before Moses, Eleazar the priest, the leaders and the whole assembly at the entrance to the tent of meeting and said,

"Our father died in the wilderness. He was not among Korah's followers, who banded together against the Lord, but he died for his own sin and left no sons. Why should our father's name disappear from his clan because he had no son? Give us property among our father's relatives."

So Moses brought their case before the Lord, and the Lord said to him, "What Zelophehad's daughters are saying is right. You must certainly give them property as an inheritance among their father's relatives and give their father's inheritance to them.

"Say to the Israelites, 'If a man dies and leaves no son, give his inheritance to his daughter. If he has no daughter, give his inheritance to his brothers. If he has no brothers, give his inheritance to his father's brothers. If his father had no brothers, give his inheritance to the nearest relative in his clan, that he may possess it. This is to have the force of law for the Israelites, as the Lord commanded Moses'" (Num. 27:1-11).

Acts of Intercession

The Women's Rights movement started long before the 1920s! The Zelophehad sisters made history by pleading their case to Moses. The sister's father had died a natural death, and they had no brothers to claim his inheritance of the land that was granted to him when they arrived to the Promise Land.

At this time, under Hebrew law, only sons had rights to claim their father's inheritance. The sisters went to Moses and pleaded their case to have access to what was promised to their father. In doing this, Moses had to go to God and inquire about what should be done. God told Moses to give them the land and rewrite the law.

These five sisters had the courage to speak up in spite of the law and tradition that was currently in place. They could have said nothing and walked away. There are many divorced women today and many who have never been married but have children. The Zelophehad sisters were single ladies with no father, brother, or husband to take care of them. During this time in history women had little or no rights.

The lesson that we can learn as women is that we need to recognize our influence in our family, our community, our local, state, and national government. We have a united voice to bring positive change into everyone's life (man or woman). If we live in a nation that allows women to vote, we need to be sure that we are exercising our right.

Maybe you are in a country were women do not have any rights to vote or enjoy the same privileges that men do. I encourage you to not give up hope. Continue to let your faith be strong in God and obey everything that He has for you to do. The sisters were on one accord for a specific purpose.

Isn't it amazing what we can get accomplished if we work together for a common cause? The sisters had the courage to challenge tradition, go speak to Moses, (the spiritual and political leader of the nation of Israel at the time), and plead their case for their family. Because of their courage not only was their family affected in the present, the law was changed for the future.

Application, Thoughts & Questions

Questions

1. What social economic challenges are you, someone you know, and/or women around the world facing today?

_____
_____
_____
_____
_____
_____
_____ .
_____

2. How can we come together more as women to make a change in the world?

_____
_____
_____
_____
_____
_____
_____
_____

Chapter 9
Rahab

Rahab's act of intercession was her faith in God through the risky actions she took. Her actions saved her and her family from destruction.

Rahab

Then Joshua son of Nun secretly sent two spies from Shittim. "Go, look over the land," he said, "especially Jericho." So they went and entered the house of a prostitute named Rahab and stayed there.

The king of Jericho was told, "Look, some of the Israelites have come here tonight to spy out the land." So the king of Jericho sent this message to Rahab: "Bring out the men who came to you and entered your house, because they have come to spy out the whole land."

But the woman had taken the two men and hidden them. She said, "Yes, the men came to me, but I did not know where they had come from. At dusk, when it was time to close the city gate, they left. I don't know which way they went. Go after them quickly. You may catch up with them." (But she had taken them up to the roof and hidden them under the stalks of flax she had laid out on the roof.)

So the men set out in pursuit of the spies on the road that leads to the fords of the Jordan, and as soon as the pursuers had gone out, the gate was shut. Before the spies lay down for the night, she went up on the roof and said to them, "I know that the Lord has given you this land and that a great fear of you has fallen on us, so that all who live in this country are melting in fear because of you.

We have heard how the Lord dried up the water of the Red Sea for you when you came out of Egypt, and what you did to Sihon and Og, the two kings of the Amorites east of the Jordan, whom you completely destroyed. When we heard of it, our hearts melted in fear and everyone's courage failed because of you, for the Lord your

Acts of Intercession

God is God in heaven above and on the earth below.

"Now then, please swear to me by the Lord that you will show kindness to my family, because I have shown kindness to you. Give me a sure sign that you will spare the lives of my father and mother, my brothers and sisters, and all who belong to them —and that you will save us from death."

"Our lives for your lives!" the men assured her. "If you don't tell what we are doing, we will treat you kindly and faithfully when the Lord gives us the land.

Joshua said to the two men who had spied out the land, "Go into the prostitute's house and bring her out and all who belong to her, in accordance with your oath to her." So the young men who had done the spying went in and brought out Rahab, her father and mother, her brothers and sisters and all who belonged to her. They brought out her entire family and put them in a place outside the camp of Israel (Josh. 2:1-14, 6:22-23).

What is the first word or image that comes to your mind when you think of a prostitute? It may not be positive. I am glad that we serve a God who does not think like us. He is able to take a negative situation and turn it around for His glory. Rahab is a great example of how God can use anyone regardless of who they are and what they do.

Rahab was a woman of influence. She was a prostitute by profession, but what God had for her and her family was greater than her current situation.

Here were the negative factors that surrounded her:

a) She was a prostitute,

b) She lived in Jericho, a city that worshipped idol gods,

c) The people in the city lived in fear on a daily basis,

d) The city was "shut up",

e) Her family's wellbeing depended on her profession,

f) Due to her profession, she was looked upon in society as low class, and

g) She was a woman living in a time where women did not have very many rights.

We may not be living in the same situation as Rahab, but we can relate to not being dealt the "best hand". For example, we may come from a very dysfunctional family. Or, maybe our parents never taught us about God or lived Godly lives. Some of us were born into poverty and our family has a poverty mentality.

Maybe we have made some bad choices such as prostitution, abortion, drugs, bad relationships, bullying, etc. Some of us may live in a Jericho-like area where people live in fear, or there is nothing good coming in or going out of the neighborhood. Whatever the situation, God is still faithful and He uses people like Rahab to get His will accomplished in earth.

God does not care about what we've done, where we live,

Acts of Intercession

or what the world thinks about us. He moves on our faith towards him. Rahab did not grow up in a city where the true and living God was recognized or worshiped. Yet, by Rahab heard about all God had done for the Israelites', and it activated her faith to trust and believe that God would work on her and her families' behalf.

What was so special about Rahab? All the inhabitants of Jericho were living day to day in fear of the Israelites coming, to the point they had shut up the city; no one could to go in or out. Instead of living in fear, Rahab was given the opportunity–through the spies coming to her house, to bless God's people instead of live in fear of them. She risked her and her families' lives to help the spies accomplish their mission.

Application, Thoughts & Questions

Application

The lesson that we can learn from Rahab is not to let our current situation define who we are. We are everything God has called us to be. Rahab is in the lineage of our Lord and Savior Jesus Christ. We are all carrying a seed that will one day be greater than us. God can and will use anyone that He pleases. Rahab was labeled a prostitute by the world's standard, but by God's standard she was a daughter of the most high...and so are you!

Questions

1. Have you ever been judged by other people because of who you are or what you do? How did it make you feel?

_____

_____

_____

_____

_____

_____

2. If you know that your lifestyle is not pleasing to God and you want to change, write out a prayer request to God.

_____

_____

_____

_____

_____

3. Rahab's decision to trust God impacted her whole family in a positive way. What are some things that you are doing now to impact your family's wellbeing?

_____
_____
_____
_____
_____
_____

Chapter 10
Deborah

Deborah's act of intercession was her leadership over Israel as a judge.

Deborah

Now Deborah, a prophet, the wife of Lappidoth, was leading Israel at that time. She held court under the Palm of Deborah between Ramah and Bethel in the hill country of Ephraim, and the Israelites went up to her to have their disputes decided. She sent for Barak son of Abinoam from Kedesh in Naphtali and said to him, "The Lord, the God of Israel, commands you: 'Go, take with you ten thousand men of Naphtali and Zebulun and lead them up to Mount Tabor. I will lead Sisera, the commander of Jabin's army, with his chariots and his troops to the Kishon River and give him into your hands.'"

Barak said to her, "If you go with me, I will go; but if you don't go with me, I won't go."

"Certainly I will go with you," said Deborah. "But because of the course you are taking, the honor will not be yours, for the Lord will deliver Sisera into the hands of a woman."

So Deborah went with Barak to Kedesh. There Barak summoned Zebulun and Naphtali, and ten thousand men went up under his command. Deborah also went up with him. Now Heber the Kenite had left the other Kenites, the descendants of Hobab, Moses' brother-in-law, and pitched his tent by the great tree in Zaanannim near Kedesh.

When they told Sisera that Barak son of Abinoam had gone up to Mount Tabor, Sisera summoned from Harosheth Haggoyim to the Kishon River all his men and his nine hundred chariots fitted with iron.

Then Deborah said to Barak, "Go! This is the day the Lord has given Sisera into your hands. Has not the Lord gone ahead of you?"

So Barak went down Mount Tabor, with ten thousand men following him. At Barak's advance, the Lord routed Sisera and all his chariots and army by the sword, and Sisera got down from his chariot and fled on foot.

Barak pursued the chariots and army as far as Harosheth Haggoyim, and all Sisera's troops fell by the sword; not a man was left (Judges 4:4-16).

Deborah was a wife, homemaker, prophetess, judge, community leader, warrior, praise and worshipper, spiritual advisor, mother figure, military advisor, and mentor. She made history in Israel by becoming the first female judge. Deborah had national influence.

She was a judge with a two-folded responsibility. She had to settle disputes within the community, and she was the spiritual leader of Israel. During this time Israel did not have a king to lead them, God lead them, and the judges delivered the messages from God. Deborah was the one who started the war with the Canaanites when she summoned Barak to go out and lead the army of Israel. She also went physically with Barak into battle and advised Barak on when his troops were to attack the enemy.

Deborah was a praise and worshipper of God. She spoke the things of God, judged according to the Word of God and used her earthly influence to bring glory to Him. She even had a song of praise:

Acts of Intercession

On that day Deborah and Barak son of Abinoam sang this song:

"When the princes in Israel take the lead,
when the people willingly offer themselves—praise the Lord!
"Hear this, you kings! Listen, you rulers! I, even I, will sing to
the Lord;
I will praise the Lord, the God of Israel, in song.

"When you, Lord, went out from Seir,
when you marched from the land of Edom, the earth shook, the
heavens poured, the clouds poured down water.
The mountains quaked before the Lord, the One of Sinai,
before the Lord, the God of Israel.

"In the days of Shamgar son of Anath,
in the days of Jael, the highways were abandoned;
travelers took to winding paths.
Villagers in Israel would not fight;
they held back until I, Deborah, arose,
until I arose, a mother in Israel.
God chose new leaders
when war came to the city gates,
but not a shield or spear was seen
among forty thousand in Israel.
My heart is with Israel's princes,
with the willing volunteers among the people.

Praise the Lord! "You who ride on white donkeys,
sitting on your saddle blankets,
and you who walk along the road,
consider 11 the voice of the singers at the watering places.

They recite the victories of the Lord,
the victories of his villagers in Israel.

"Then the people of the Lord
went down to the city gates.
'Wake up, wake up, Deborah!
Wake up, wake up, break out in song!
Arise, Barak!
Take captive your captives, son of Abinoam.'

"The remnant of the nobles came down;
the people of the Lord came down to me against the mighty
(Judges 5:1-13).

I included this song of praise (in decrees) in this chapter because I want you to understand the importance of praise after your victory. We must make sure we always acknowledge God in everything because it is He who gives us the victory for His glory.

Praise is a sign of our gratitude towards God. It helps us take the focus off ourselves and put it on Him. Deborah recapped in detailed everything that God had done for Israel in the battle. The next time you are going through a rough period in your life, think back, in detail, on what God has brought you through until this point.

Through it all, she had to have balance in her life to be able to manage her spiritual and earthly calling. Deborah was the wife to Lappidoth. I like that the chapter starts out stating that, because it speaks volumes. As women, we are called to be and do many things. But, if we have the responsibility of marriage, home is our first and most important responsibility and ministry. If our home life is balanced, it will help balance everything else–whether you are married or single.

I can relate to Deborah because I am a wife, mother, preacher, church leader, nurse, mentor, and business-woman. I found that I have to prioritize my responsibilities in order to be effective in my gifting and callings.

How are you balancing your time daily as it relates to your calling? If you do not have balance in your life, pray to God to show you what you need to do, and obey His instructions immediately.

Deborah used her influence in a positive way. The whole nation of Israel was listening to her praise report. She made sure that when the spotlight was on her, she gave God the praise. This praise gave hope, courage, and strengthened faith in the hearts of people who had been suppressed for twenty years. This praise helped turn the hearts of the people back to God.

For the believers reading this text, think about the last time you praised or testified about God publicly. Was the praise focused on you or God? Did it influence anyone else to praise God? Did your praise give hope, courage, or faith to someone else? What are some things that you praise God for?

Chapter 11
Jael

Jael's act of intercession was through her action of killing Sisera. It was a turning point in Israel's quest toward independence from the Canaanites.

Sisera, meanwhile, fled on foot to the tent of Jael, the wife of Heber the Kenite, because there was an alliance between Jabin king of Hazor and the family of Heber the Kenite. Jael went out to meet Sisera and said to him, "Come, my lord, come right in. Don't be afraid." So he entered her tent, and she covered him with a blanket.

"I'm thirsty," he said. "Please give me some water." She opened a skin of milk, gave him a drink, and covered him up. "Stand in the doorway of the tent," he told her. "If someone comes by and asks you, 'Is anyone in there?' say 'No.'"

But Jael, Heber's wife, picked up a tent peg and a hammer and went quietly to him while he lay fast asleep, exhausted. She drove the peg through his temple into the ground, and he died.

Just then Barak came by in pursuit of Sisera, and Jael went out to meet him. "Come," she said, "I will show you the man you're looking for." So he went in with her, and there lay Sisera with the tent peg through his temple—dead (Judges 4:17-22, 5:24-30).

"Most blessed of women be Jael, the wife of Heber the Kenite, most blessed of tent-dwelling women. He asked for water, and she gave him milk; in a bowl fit for nobles she brought him curdled milk. Her hand reached for the tent peg, her right hand for the workman's hammer. She struck Sisera, she crushed his head, she shattered and pierced his temple. At her feet he sank, he fell; there he lay. At her feet he sank, he fell; where he sank, there he fell—dead. "Through the window peered Sisera's mother; behind the lattice she cried out, 'Why is his chariot so long in

coming? Why is the clatter of his chariots delayed?' The wisest of her ladies answer her; indeed, she keeps saying to herself, 'Are they not finding and dividing the spoils: a woman or two for each man, colorful garments as plunder for Sisera, colorful garments embroidered, highly embroidered garments for my neck—all this as plunder (Judges 5:24-30).

During this time in Israel's history, King Jabin (a Canaanite King) had been ruling over Israel, through his army's commander Sisera. For twenty years he ruled over the Israelites who had sinned against God. The nation of Israel cried out to the Lord for help and God raised up a woman judge named Deborah. Deborah was an instrumental leader who helped to bring forth the revolution of Israel's freedom from King Jabin.

Barak was the commander of Israel's army who asked Deborah to go with him and his army into battle (even though she had told him God would be with him). Deborah agreed, but she told him that the victory would go into the hands of a woman. Boy, did her prophecy come true!

Jael was a warrior in her own right. She was not physically on the battlefield with the men, but she knew how to protect the home front. She was a woman who knew how to pitch a tent–which in those days was equivalent to our mobile homes of today.

To pitch a tent required skill, expertise and strength. Jael was married to Heber. Heber was neutral with his allegiance to Israel and the Cannonities, but Jael had a mind of her own. And it was made up. She had unspoken allegiance with the army of Israel through her interaction with Sisera.

Acts of Intercession

The Israelite army killed all of Sisera's troops. Sisera however escaped and ran by the tent of Jael for his safety. Jael took advantage of the situation and invited him into her tent where she treated him kindly. However, in the back of her head she was plotting to kill him. Jael killed Sisera by driving a stake through his head while he was sleep. When Barak came looking for him, she said, "Come over here I have what you are looking for."

Wow! From a modern-day world point of view we would label her a murderer, ruthless, heartless, gangster, sociopathic, and cold-blooded. But we have to remember that this happened during time of war. Israel was regaining their independence from the Canaanites who were idol worshipping with no respect for the true and living God. It was time to take a stand against the enemy who had been suppressing them for twenty years.

Jael had the courage to be fearless in the presence of the enemy. She killed the leader of the Canaanite army. This was a huge statement because, as a woman (who in those days did not have many rights) she did a "man's job." It was shameful for a man to lose his life to a woman. While women warriors are not mentioned in the Bible, Jael made history when she executed the head army general of the Canaanites.

Jael knew the enemy, and his name was Sisera. When it was time to annihilate him she did so swiftly, without hesitation. We can take a lesson from her when it comes to fighting Satan. When sin comes to our house, we do not need to invite it in or give it a safe haven. We need to get rid of it immediately before it becomes detrimental to our lives, our community, and our nation.

You may be going through a rough period in life where you think the enemy has you bound. Take a lesson from Jael; you are stronger than you think. Have the courage to stop the enemy in his tracks. You have access to living a life of freedom through Jesus Christ. He defeated the enemy a long time ago on Calvary, and you can defeat the enemy today through Christ blood. Give your life to God and let Him fight your battles.

Application, Thoughts & Questions

Application

Jael's act of killing Sisera impacted the whole nation of Israel. It gave them the courage that they needed to defeat an enemy that had been suppressing them for twenty years. Realize today that every time you resist the enemy that you're impacting the lives of others for the better.

Questions

1. Israel benefited from Jael killing Sisera. It gave them hope that they could defeat the Canaanites that had been oppressing them for so long. Who are some of the "Jael's" in your life who have given you hope?

_____

_____

_____

_____

_____

2. Jael was able to take advantage of an opportunity of a lifetime, by Sisera coming to her house. She made a split decision that changed the course of Israel's history. What opportunities have come your way that you took advantage of because of it changed your life and the life of others?

_____

_____

_____

_____

Chapter 12

Samson's Mother

Samson's mother (and father's) act of intercession was obeying all the instructions that were given to her regarding the care of Samson.

Samson's Mother

A certain man of Zorah, named Manoah, from the clan of the Danites, had a wife who was childless, unable to give birth. The angel of the Lord appeared to her and said:

"You are barren and childless, but you are going to become pregnant and give birth to a son. Now see to it that you drink no wine or other fermented drink and that you do not eat anything unclean. You will become pregnant and have a son whose head is never to be touched by a razor because the boy is to be a Nazirite, dedicated to God from the womb. He will take the lead in delivering Israel from the hands of the Philistines."

Then the woman went to her husband and told him, "A man of God came to me. He looked like an angel of God, very awesome. I didn't ask him where he came from, and he didn't tell me his name. But he said to me, 'You will become pregnant and have a son. Now then, drink no wine or other fermented drink and do not eat anything unclean, because the boy will be a Nazirite of God from the womb until the day of his death.'"

Then Manoah prayed to the Lord: "Pardon your servant, Lord. I beg you to let the man of God you sent to us come again to teach us how to bring up the boy who is to be born." God heard Manoah, and the angel of God came again to the woman while she was out in the field; but her husband Manoah was not with her. The woman hurried to tell her husband, "He's here! The man who appeared to me the other day!"

Manoah got up and followed his wife. When he came to the man, he said, "Are you the man who talked to my wife?" "I am," he said. So Manoah asked him, "When your words are fulfilled, what is to be the rule that governs the boy's life and work?"

The angel of the Lord answered, "Your wife must do all that I have told her. She must not eat anything that comes from the grapevine, nor drink any wine or other fermented drink nor eat anything unclean. She must do everything I have commanded her."

Manoah said to the angel of the Lord, "We would like you to stay until we prepare a young goat for you." The angel of the Lord replied, "Even though you detain me, I will not eat any of your food. But if you prepare a burnt offering, offer it to the Lord." (Manoah did not realize that it was the angel of the Lord. Then Manoah inquired of the angel of the Lord, "What is your name, so that we may honor you when your word comes true?"
He replied, "Why do you ask my name? It is beyond understanding."

Then Manoah took a young goat, together with the grain offering, and sacrificed it on a rock to the Lord. And the Lord did an amazing thing while Manoah and his wife watched: As the flame blazed up from the altar toward heaven, the angel of the Lord ascended in the flame. Seeing this, Manoah and his wife fell with their faces to the ground. When the angel of the Lord did not show himself again to Manoah and his wife, Manoah realized that it was the angel of the Lord.

"We are doomed to die!" he said to his wife. "We have seen God!" But his wife answered, "If the Lord had meant to kill us, he would not have accepted a burnt offering and grain offering from our hands, nor shown us all these things or now told us this." The woman gave birth to a boy and named him Samson. He grew and the Lord blessed him, *and the Spirit of the Lord began to stir him while he was in Mahaneh Dan, between Zorah and Eshtaol* (Judges 13:2-25).

Samson's birth was activated by a problem going on in the earth. The Israelites were constantly battling with the Philistines. The Philistines had a great army and they were oppressing the people of Israel. God was raising judges to lead the nation of Israel. (Israel did not have a king during this period of history.)

Samson would be a mighty warrior against the Philistines. God would use him to show off his supernatural strength against the Philistines. Although Samson would make many mistakes in his life he still was instrumental in Israel's triumph over the Philistines. Manoah's wife was infertile until God spoke (through His angel). There are women who experience physical infertility all across the world. Many may never conceive a child and others will experience having a child. In whatever situation, God is still gracious.

We should never give up on the promises God has for us. If it is His will for us to bear children, it will happen. And if it is not His will then we must accept it. It does not mean that He loves one person more than the other. It signifies the individual plan that He has for our lives.

The Bible has proven through Sarah, Rebecca, Hannah, Samson's mother, Elizabeth and many others, that God is able to bring forth a child through an infertile woman.

The child birth may have been activated by a prayer, a message from the Lord, or prophesy. The most important thing we must notice is that the activation of the conception was sparked from a Word from God.

Infertility does not have to be a physical condition; it can be spiritual as well. Many of us have dreams, visions, destinies, and most importantly purposes that we haven't fulfilled yet due to something going on in our spirit. Everything is birthed in the spirit before it manifests in the physical (here on earth). We need God to speak into our lives to activate a conception of an idea, purpose and destiny.

God knew exactly what he had in mind for Samson even before he was born. Because of the calling on Samson's life, there were special instructions given to his parents before conception. These instructions included what to do during pregnancy and how to raise him. Why would God have them follow these instructions and no one else? Sanctification is the answer. When you have been sanctified for the Lord it means you have been set apart for a special service.

It is important to note in the text that God told Manoah's wife that she could not eat anything from a grapevine. She could not have any alcoholic drink and she could not eat anything unclean. Women need to be aware of how they take care of themselves physically, spiritually, and emotionally during and after pregnancy.

What we allow to come into our bodies has an effect on our unborn child. Facts have proven that women, who do drugs and alcohol during their pregnancy, are more likely to have children with developmental problems. A healthy lifestyle before, during, and after pregnancy is beneficial to the mother and the baby. Pregnancy may not be a concern for you, but it is God's desire that we all be healthy.

God also told Samson's parents never to cut his hair. This was a tailor-made specific instruction given to them and Samson. Samson's strength was connected to his hair. Samson knew when he was grown that he was to never cut his hair. He also knew that the secret to his strength was in his hair, so he could never tell anyone about it.

When God bless us with children, we have a responsibility to them. As parents we must discern our children's gifting and talents and help to cultivate them. We need to teach them the Bible, not only through reading but through application as well. Samson's parents followed the instructions God told them, but Samson made a mistake by telling Delilah about his hair (Judges 16:17).

This is a good lesson for parents. We can raise our children with all the right values but it is still up to them to obey God for themselves. Our job is to teach them right from wrong and their job is to remember what they have been taught. Proverbs 22:6 reads: *Train up a child in the way he should go: and when he is old, he will not depart from it.*

The good thing about the story of Samson is that at the end of his life, he remembered God. He did not forget about where his strength truly came from. He prayed to God–just as his father did before, and God answered him. Just as God gave instructions for Manoah and his wife to follow, he has also given us a handbook to raise our children too…it is called the Bible.

Application, Thoughts & Questions

Application
What instructions have God specifically given you in regard to your child and the calling on their life? If you have not heard from God, pray to Him to reveal what He has for you to do.

Thought
Mahoah asked the angel to tell him his name; but his motive was wrong. He was more focused on the messenger than the message sent by God. We have to be careful how we approach God. Sometimes we ask for things that are irrelevant to our situation. We also need to make sure that our focus is on the word of God, not on *who* is bringing it.

Questions
1. Has God ever spoken to you and you were unsure it was Him? What has God told you to do that you questioned?

_____

_____

_____

_____

_____

2. What is your focus today? Is it more on man or God?

_____

_____

_____

_____

_____

3. Are you hearing the voice of God today? Do you have infertile situations going on in your life and you just need to hear a word from the Lord? If so, write below that infertile situation and a specific prayer with scriptures attached to it.

_____
_____
_____
_____
_____
_____
_____

4. Are you taking care of your body as it relates to the Word of God?

_____
_____
_____
_____
_____
_____

Chapter 13
Ruth & Naomi

Ruth's act of intercession was in her faithfulness to her mother-in-law, Naomi and in worshipping the God of Israel.

Ruth & Naomi

But Ruth replied, "Don't urge me to leave you or to turn back from you. Where you go I will go, and where you stay I will stay. Your people will be my people and your God my God" (Ruth 1:16).

The story of Ruth is about a relationship between Ruth and Naomi. Ruth was not born an Israelite but she had been married to Naomi's Israelite son. Naomi was a widow who lived with her son and daughter-in-law, Ruth. Ruth's husband died and there was a drought in the land where they were living.

Ruth and Naomi had to leave their home country because of the drought. Naomi had turned bitter because of all her circumstances and she told Ruth to leave her and go back home to her parents' house. Ruth's reply was that: "I will go wherever you go and your God will be my God."

Naomi's faith must have rubbed off on Ruth because Ruth wanted to serve the God of Naomi. Ruth was born and raised a Moabite, yet she married into a family that worshiped the God of Israel. Even when Naomi became bitter about her circumstance, Ruth still wanted to be in Naomi's life as her daughter-in-law. She did not want to leave her mother-in-law alone when times got rough.

Ruth and Naomi's mutual connection was through Ruth's husband. Once he died they could have went their separate ways. But a bond was already formed between them through the mutual recognition of God in their lives.

Bitter people are sometimes the hardest people to get along with. They tend to be pessimistic instead of optimistic. Their hope for future tends to be dim because they cannot get over their past.

Let us remember Ruth's response to her bitter mother-in-law. She did not abandon her because of the mental state she was in. Instead of running in the opposite direction, she vowed to stay with her and worship God.

Ruth and Naomi were facing a drought (hunger), homelessness, no financial support, no other immediate family to support them, and uncertainty of the conditions of where they were going. Yet by Ruth's statement of "where ever you go I will go and your God will be my God", was seed planted into her and her families future. She had faith that God was going to see them through, and He did.

Together they traveled to Jerusalem where Naomi had distant relatives. They worked in the fields of Boaz who soon took a liking to Ruth. Ruth eventually married Boaz and in their lineage would be King David and Jesus Christ.

Application, Thoughts & Questions

Application
Acknowledgement of God when we are going through difficult times will help us get through them. Worship will give us the supernatural strength to make it through some of the darkest periods in our life. Let this be a lesson to us when we are faced with hardships and the uncertainties of life. Let us speak on the God we serve rather than the problems we face.

Thought
Your faith in God has influence on other people placed in your life. We must remember that family is more than blood relation; family is about relationship. Relationships are often tested through various obstacles and hardships. When God is the center of your worship it helps you get through tough trails as a family.

Questions
1. Can you think of someone in your family (non-blood related or related) whose faith inspired you to want to keep going when you experienced rough times in your life? Who were they? How did they inspire you?

_____
_____
_____
_____
_____

_____
_____
_____

We may not be able to physically be with our loved ones who have reached a bitter point in their lives, but we can pray for them and speak life to them. Write a prayer for someone you know who is going through a rough time in life.

_____
_____
_____
_____
_____

Write some hardships that you are facing right now, and then write what God can do through them.

_____
_____
_____
_____
_____
_____
_____
_____
_____

Chapter 14
Hannah

Hannah's act of intercession was praying for her unborn child and dedicating him to God.

Hannah

Once when they had finished eating and drinking in Shiloh, Hannah stood up. Now Eli the priest was sitting on his chair by the door post of the Lord's house. In her deep anguish Hannah prayed to the Lord, weeping bitterly. And she made a vow, saying, "Lord Almighty, if you will only look on your servant's misery and remember me, and not forget your servant but give her a son, then I will give him to the Lord for all the days of his life, and no razor will ever be used on his head."

Eli answered, "Go in peace, and may the God of Israel grant you what you have asked of him."

Early the next morning they arose and worshiped before the Lord and then went back to their home at Ramah. Elkanah made love to his wife Hannah and the Lord remembered her. So in the course of time Hannah became pregnant and gave birth to a son. She named him Samuel, saying, "Because I asked the Lord for him" (1 Samuel 1:9-11, 17, 19-20).

Prayer changes things!

Hannah's prayer was birthed out of years of infertility and torment from her husband's other wife, Peninnah. Hannah was bullied because she was infertile. Peninnah (who had children) would use Hannah's infertility to harass and taunt her.

Every year the whole family would worship God at the temple, according to their custom. This particular year Hannah prayed to God–through her misery and pain, for a child. She stated that if He blessed her with a child she would dedicate him back to God.

Bullying has been around since biblical days. Hannah's bullying came from Peninnah being jealous that her husband loved Hannah more. Peninnah was able to give him children but his affection went toward Hannah. Peninnah used Hannah's weakness against her. She saw that it really bothered Hannah that she could not have children, and she played on it to the point Hannah became depressed and bitter.

To overcome bullies, we need to bring the problem to God through prayer and action. Bullying can be physical and emotional, many times leaving people scarred for life. There is a phrase that states, "hurt people hurt people." That was the case between Peninnah and Hannah. Peninnah wanted her husband's love and affection, (which Hannah got) but Hannah wanted a child, (which Peninnah got).

Bullies are not born to be bullies, but the spirit comes about through something that they are lacking within themselves. They pick on the weakness of others to make themselves feel superficially better or superior. Hannah was in deep anguish and she was weeping bitterly when she prayed. Years of bullying had brought her to this place in her life.

She cried out to God from a place of deep hurt and God heard her prayer. We may or may not have experienced bullying, but we all may have had deep hurt in our lives. Hannah had to push past her pain and make her request to God about her issue of infertility. She did not go to him complaining about Peninnah. She went to him requesting deliverance from her barrenness. She prayed about her weakness not for deliverance from her adversary.

God did answer her prayer and she gave birth to a son named Samuel. Within Hannah's prayer request, she stated that if the Lord blessed her with a son, that she would dedicate him back to God. Samuel had a special calling on his life. He was a prophet of God who had to anoint the first two kings of Israel. Hannah did not know how God was going to use Samuel during this period in the history of Israel, but God knew his destiny.

It is so important for mothers to pray for their children. Our simple prayers are connected to getting them where they need to be. We help them to fulfill their God-given purpose. Hannah stated that she would dedicate him to God and she did just what she promised.

We should all dedicate our children to God if we believe in Him and His word. God chooses us to be parents. We must always remember that our children belong to Him first before He gave them to us. We all belong to God and we must live a dedicated life to Him.

Application, Thoughts & Questions

Application

When we are going through difficult times, we need to remember the God we serve. God is the one who gives life, not man. It doesn't matter who is against you, if God is for you.

Questions

1. Have you ever been bullied, or has someone else ever deliberately mistreated you for no reason? What were the results of it? What was your response? Lastly have you forgiven them?

_____
_____
_____
_____
_____
_____

2. Our children may not go and serve in the house of the Lord like Samuel did, but we can teach them how to serve and worship the Lord. What values are you instilling in your children as it relates to your dedication to God?

_____
_____
_____
_____
_____
_____
_____
_____

Write a prayer for your child/children and/or unborn child. If you are having infertility issues, write a prayer for it.

_____
_____
_____
_____
_____
_____
_____
_____
_____
_____
_____

Do you have a weakness that you need to bring to God? Do you need help overcoming your adversary? If you are experiencing deep hurt and pain, like Hannah, write a prayer.

_____
_____
_____
_____
_____
_____
_____
_____
_____
_____
_____

Chapter 15
Michal

Michal's act of intercession was helping David escape from a death threat made by her father.

Michal

Saul sent men to David's house to watch it and to kill him in the morning. But Michal, David's wife, warned him, "If you don't run for your life tonight, tomorrow you'll be killed."

So Michal let David down through a window, and he fled and escaped. Then Michal took an idol and laid it on the bed, covering it with a garment and putting some goats' hair at the head (1 Samuel 19:11-13).

Michal was the daughter of Saul, who was the first king of Israel. Saul gave Michal to David in marriage. Saul was like a father to David, but as time went on Saul became extremely jealous of him. (Saul was jealous of David because Saul has recently lost his anointing of God and David had God's anointing). Saul also had a tormenting spirit living within him, which led him to despise David.

Michal was caught in the middle of her father and David, the future king. I am sure she loved them both but this text clearly shows her loyalty more to her husband than her father. She knew that Saul wanted to kill her husband unjustly. She knew that she had to help David escape the murderous plot that was placed on his life. Not only did she help him escape she covered for him as well by making a fake impression of a sleeping David in their bed.

When you are married your spouse becomes your top priority. No one should have more influence over you than your spouse–not even your own parents. I am not saying to disrespect your parents or push them to the side when you get married, but once you are married your obligation is no longer to your parents, it's to your spouse. God chooses who our mother and father are going to be. Some of us were raised in two parent homes; others have been raised in single parent homes. Some of us may not know our mother or father. Some of us were brought up in homes that functioned "normally", and others have been raised in dysfunction.

In this story Michal's father, King Saul, was living a life in torment. In today's terms, he had become mentally ill. Mental illness within the family, especially coming from the head of the household will cause dysfunction in the house. Here is a synopsis of Saul's mental status at this time and his view on Michal and David's relationship:

In the meantime, Saul's daughter Michal had fallen in love with David, and Saul was delighted when he heard about it. Here's another chance to see him killed by the Philistines! Saul said to himself. But to David he said, "Today you will have a second chance to be my son-in-law!"(1 Samuel 18:20-21).

Saul used his daughter Michal's hand in marriage as a pawn to try to get David killed. He wanted David to go and fight the Philistines and bring back 100 foreskins of their heads for Michal's hand in marriage. He thought David would lose his life in battle, but with God's help David brought back 200 foreskins.

In 1 Samuel 18:28-29, Saul realized that the Lord was with David and how much his daughter Michal loved him. Saul became even more afraid of him and remained David's enemy for the rest of his life.

Michal's father Saul was dealing with several internal issues:

* He had lost the anointing of God by sinning against Him,

* God had sent Saul a tormenting spirit of depression and fear (1 Sam. 16:14),

* Saul would lose his temper in violent fits of rage,

*Saul became very jealous of David to the point he wanted him dead, and

*Saul realized that his daughter truly loved David and he felt that her love for David was a betrayal to him (1 Sam. 19:17).

I could only imagine how Michal internalized this. Some of us have had to deal with parents or loved ones who do not live their lives pleasing to God. Saul could have made better decisions and choices, but because his heart had turned from God, he failed.

Michal could have chosen to follow in the steps of her father, but because of love, she didn't. Michal had fallen in love with David. Loving someone and being in love with someone are two different things. Just *loving* someone can be superficial and it often comes with conditions. When you are *in love* with someone they have your heart no matter what the situation or circumstance; it is unconditional.

The Bible states that love covers a multitude of sins. Saul was walking in sin and his love for Michal had conditions attach to it. Michal's love for David was unconditional; and her love brought forth David life. Obviously, Michal loved

David and she would not let him be killed by her own father and his evil ways. Her actions showed her loyalty, strength and courage to her marriage to David.

Growing up in dysfunctional homes can leave physical, spiritual, and emotional scars on our lives. Depending on the circumstances that we had to endure, it can have a traumatic negative effect in our lives and our relationships with other people. God can heal the brokenness inside if we let him.

Love saved David's life and love can do the same for us. God has given us love through His son Jesus Christ, but we have to accept him. It is through the understanding of love sacrificed on the cross that helps us in our time of need. The love that was displayed on the cross teaches us how to forgive the ones who have hurt us, love the ones who are hard to love, and receive true love, which is unconditional.

Application, Thoughts & Questions

Question

1. Have you experienced dysfunction within your family? How did it affect you and/or internalize it?

_____
_____
_____
_____
_____
_____

If you have experienced a parent, family member, friend, co-worker, etc. who suffered from internal issues such as mental illness, making poor decisions, or they are just have wicked ways, write a prayer for them below. Remember the unconditional love that God has for us; write your prayer out of love for them.

_____
_____
_____
_____
_____
_____
_____
_____
_____

Have you forgiven your family members who have hurt you from their own personal dysfunctional ways? Why or why not? If your answer is no, ask Jesus to come into your heart and heal you from the pain of your past.

Chapter 16
Abigail

Abigail's act of intercession was asking for forgiveness of her husband's wicked ways.

Abigail

When Abigail saw David, she quickly got off her donkey and bowed down before David with her face to the ground. She fell at his feet and said:

"Pardon your servant, my lord, and let me speak to you; hear what your servant has to say. Please pay no attention, my lord, to that wicked man Nabal. He is just like his name—his name means Fool, and folly goes with him. And as for me, your servant, I did not see the men my lord sent. And now, my lord, as surely as the Lord your God lives and as you live, since the Lord has kept you from blood-shed and from avenging yourself with your own hands, may your enemies and all who are intent on harming my lord be like Nabal. And let this gift, which your servant has brought to my lord, be given to the men who follow you.

"Please forgive your servant's presumption. The Lord your God will certainly make a lasting dynasty for my lord, because you fight the Lord's battles, and no wrongdoing will be found in you as long as you live. Even though someone is pursuing you to take your life, the life of my lord will be bound securely in the bundle of the living by the Lord your God, but the lives of your enemies he will hurl away as from the pocket of a sling.

When the Lord has fulfilled for my lord every good thing he promised concerning him and has appointed him ruler over Israel, my lord will not have on his conscience the staggering burden of needless bloodshed or of having avenged himself. And when the Lord your God has brought my lord success, remember your servant."

Acts of Intercession

David said to Abigail,

"Praise be to the Lord, the God of Israel, who has sent you today to meet me. May you be blessed for your good judgment and for keeping me from bloodshed this day and from avenging myself with my own hands. Otherwise, as surely as the Lord, the God of Israel, lives, who has kept me from harming you, if you had not come quickly to meet me, not one male belonging to Nabal would have been left alive by daybreak."

Then David accepted from her hand what she had brought him and said, "Go home in peace. I have heard your words and granted your request."

When Abigail went to Nabal, he was in the house holding a banquet like that of a king. He was in high spirits and very drunk. So she told him nothing at all until daybreak. Then in the morning, when Nabal was sober, his wife told him all these things, and his heart failed him and he became like a stone. About ten days later, the Lord struck Nabal and he died (1 Samuel 25:23-38).

Abigail was married to a man who made very foolish and wicked decisions. The Bible states that he was a wealthy man, but crude and mean in all his dealings. He was proud, stingy, and arrogant and he liked to insult people.

David and his men were in the wilderness at this time, and they guarded and showed kindness to Nabal's servants while they were shepherding in the fields. One day David sent a request to Nabal for provisions for himself and his men. Nabal sent back a message of insult to David even though he knew that David and his men had been good to his servants. David prepared to go kill Nabal and his family.

Abigail received word of what her husband did and she immediately took action. She had her servants pack up the provisions that David had requested and brought them to him. When she arrived where David and his men were she acknowledge him as a man of God and she apologized for her husband's wrong doing. She also spoke blessings over his life.

Many women around the world are living in bad marriages. Abigail was married to a foolish wicked man. The story does not give us details about how she was treated in the marriage, but it does show us how he treated other people. Nabal was the kind of man who wanted all the attention. He did not want to supply David and his men the provisions that they requested, but he was able to throw a banquet at his house "like that of a king". He had no problem showing off his wealth and being generous to those at the party, because his motive stemmed from pride and selfishness.

If you are in a marriage, and your husband does not honor God, or God's people, you should gleam from this story. Abigail chose to display righteousness even though her husband did not. She chose wisdom over foolishness. Unlike her husband, she chose to make righteous decisions that impacted her household in a positive way.

We live in a day and time now where we do not have to stay in bad marriages; we can get a divorce and move on. Yet, for the believers in God, divorce should never be the first option, it should be the last.

Acts of Intercession

Now, I will speak to the rest of you–though I do not have a direct command from the Lord. If a Christian man has a wife who is not a believer and she is willing to continue living with him, he must not leave her. And if a Christian woman has a husband who is not a believer and he is willing to continue living with her, she must not leave him. For the Christian wife brings holiness to her marriage, and the Christian husband bring holiness to the marriage (1 Cor. 7:12-14).

Wives must realize that their husbands might be saved because of them. Husbands also must realize that their wives might be saved because of them as well.

Salvation will bring restoration to spouses and marriages. The only Bible some unbelieving spouses will "read" is their spouse and their actions within the marriage. Abigail did not give up on her husband; rather she interceded for him.

Prayer can change bad situations and people. Nabal was wealthy physically but poor spiritually. Abigail knew his weakness, but she was strong for the family in her wisdom. She knew that if she did not do something to intervene, there was going to be severe punishment brought upon her household. It was through Abigail's quick act of intercession, that her life and those in household were spared.

Her actions proved that she was a woman of integrity, good and moral character, and most importantly, wisdom. Abigail also was a woman of discernment. She did not tell Nabal what she had done until the next day–after he sobered up from partying the night before. She wanted Nabal to be able to hear and understand the what she was about to tell him without any interference from the substance of alcohol. In any relationship–especially marriage–we must be able to discern the best time to talk about serious issues going on in the relationship. When you are dealing with a spouse or anyone who does not practice righteousness, it is important to know how to communicate with them. Timing is everything.

Nabal received the word from Abigail and he also received his judgment from God through her word. Nabal had a stroke and died ten days later. Illnesses can come upon us because of our disobedience. Nabal was already spiritually ill and the illness manifested itself through his actions and decisions. Abigail's righteousness caused her to speak with authority and God used her to bring forth justice.

When Nabal died, David made Abigail his wife. Abigail's marriage to David was a blessing from God. She was use to living in abundance through the wealth of her husband Nabal, but the price of the lavish living was being married to a fool. Nabal's love of money and power, pride, and arrogance lead to his demise. Abigail choosing to honor the man of God with her wealth led to a better life and future.

Marrying David (who was King of Israel) not only gave her wealth and prestige, but it gave her security in knowing that she was marrying a God-fearing righteous man. We do not know what Abigail had to endure in her marriage to Nabal, but we do know that she honored God and his people and she was blessed because of it.

Application, Thoughts & Questions

Thought

I do not condone staying in an abusive relationship. If your spouse is physically, mentally, or emotionally abusing you on a repeated basis, and they refuse to change then you may have to leave for the well being of you and your household. Many women have lost their lives in abusive relationships because they thought their spouse would change. We can pray for our spouse to change, but ultimately they have to want to change. God can and will work in our lives, but we have to give Him permission to do so because He gave us all free will.

If you, or someone you know is in a bad marriage or relationship write out a prayer, remembering the wisdom and action of Abigail.

_____
_____
_____
_____
_____
_____
_____
_____
_____
_____
_____
_____
_____
_____
_____

Questions

1. Does Abigail's story inspire you? If so, how?

_____

_____

_____

_____

_____

2. Think of a time where you had to use wisdom to get yourself or your family out of a bad situation. What was the outcome? Now think of a time when you did not use wisdom in a bad situation, what was that outcome?

_____

_____

_____

_____

_____

_____

If you were unable to answer the question above meditate on James 1:5 (KJV) _If any of you lack wisdom, let him ask God, that giveth to all men liberally, and upbraideth not; and it shall be given him._

Chapter 17
Bathsheba

Bathsheba's act of intercession was advocating for her son Solomon's kingship.

Bathsheba

Then David comforted his wife Bathsheba, and he went to her and made love to her. She gave birth to a son, and they named him Solomon. The Lord loved him; (1 Kings 1:15-21).

So Bathsheba went to see the aged king in his room, where Abishag the Shunammite was attending him. Bathsheba bowed down, prostrating herself before the king. "What is it you want?" the king asked. She said to him, "My lord, you yourself swore to me your servant by the Lord your God: 'Solomon your son shall be king after me, and he will sit on my throne.' But now Adonijah has become king, and you, my lord the king, do not know about it. He has sacrificed great numbers of cattle, fattened calves, and sheep, and has invited all the king's sons, Abiathar the priest and Joab the commander of the army, but he has not invited Solomon your servant. My lord the king, the eyes of all Israel are on you, to learn from you who will sit on the throne of my lord the king after him. Otherwise, as soon as my lord the king is laid to rest with his ancestors, I and my son Solomon will be treated as criminals" (1 Kings 1: 28-31.)

Then King David said, "Call in Bathsheba." So she came into the king's presence and stood before him. The king then took an oath: "As surely as the Lord lives, who has delivered me out of every trouble, I will surely carry out this very day what I swore to you by the Lord, the God of Israel: Solomon your son shall be king after me, and he will sit on my throne in my place." Then Bathsheba bowed down with her face to the ground, prostrating herself before the king, and said, "May my lord King David live forever!" (2 Samuel 12:24).

Bathsheba knew that her son Solomon was suppose to be king after David died. But, the current events were not unfolding in Solomon's favor. Solomon had a half brother named Adonijah, who conspired to make himself king (by self proclamation).

While King David was nearing the end of his life, Adonijah had a great ceremony to announce that he was king. He invited all his brothers, except Solomon because he knew that Solomon was the one his father David chose. He proclaimed himself king without David being aware of what was going on.

Bathsheba knew that if she did not do something Solomon was going to be robbed of his destiny. She went to the only person who had authority to change the unfolding events; she went to the King, her husband David. David immediately took action and had Solomon anointed king. When the nation of Israel heard word that Solomon had been anointed king, Adonijah's plans unraveled. He later was killed by the order of King Solomon.

We all have predetermined destinies on our lives. God knows who we are and the plans He has for us before we were ever born (Jer. 1:5). Unfortunately, sometimes we get off course in life and we do not always make it to our fullest potential. Circumstances, poor decisions and planning, and lack of knowledge can have a negative impact on our future and our purpose.

Bathsheba knew that her son was suppose to be king after David but when she received word that his half brother

Acts of Intercession

Adonijah tried to steal it from him she took immediate action. Sometimes as mothers, we have to help our children when they are unable to help themselves. We also have to know how we need to go about handling their problems without hindering their growth. We do not know how old Solomon was when he became king, but we do know that he was young in age (maybe a teenager or younger).

Bathsheba had to be a voice for Solomon because he probably was too young and inexperienced to really understand the extent of what was happening. She was the only person who was going to be able to effectively communicate to king David what was conspiring behind his back. King David made a promise to God and Bathsheba that Solomon was going to reign as king after his death. Bathsheba made sure he kept that promise.

During this period it was common for men to have multiple wives. King David had many wives and concubines. Polygamy is outlawed in most states in America, however, many Americans have siblings who do not share the same parents. Blended families are common across the world as well. King David had many children by different women and there was much dysfunction in his family. Some of the dysfunction stemmed from his sin of sleeping with another man's wife (Bathsheba), and not disciplining his children (Amnon). His son Absalom even tried to kill him for the throne. Solomon was a part of this family.

I am sure he experienced jealously, strife, and envy amongst his siblings because he was the one chosen to be the next king of Israel. Bathsheba was instrumental in Solomon's well being. Despite all the dysfunction going on in the house she was still responsible to make sure her child reached his full potential. Just like Bathsheba, we must also help our children to become the best that they can be.

We must teach them right from wrong despite the dysfunction that they may endure in their life. For example, maybe your child's father is absent from their life, or your child may have a half sibling that they do not live with or even know. Maybe you have made mistakes in your life that had a bad affect on your child. Whatever the level of dysfunction, you still have influence and can use it positively to shape their success.

Mothers can learn from Bathsheba's action of intercession for Solomon. When something is having a negative impact on a child's future, go to God with the promises of His word. Make your request based on what you know God has for your child. King David was the only someone who could put a stop to the conspiracy that was taking place in his kingdom. He was the only one who was able to speak a word to change the situation.

The word that he spoke was able to restore divine order and restoration of the kingdom to Solomon. The Word of God works the same way. When we live the Word, pray the Word, and teach our children the Word, the Word has the power to change negative situations and shape future outcomes.

Application, Thoughts & Questions

Application

Mothers and fathers need to intercede for their children. The act of intercession through prayer is great, but we need to make sure that we are living a life pleasing to God as well. It is not enough for us to pray only for our children, but we must raise them to make wise decisions.

We also must teach them how to correctly apply biblical teachings in their everyday lives through our examples. Write a prayer for each of your children accompany each prayer with scriptures of promise.

Questions

1. Have you ever had to advocate for your children before? What did you do and what were the outcomes?

_____
_____
_____
_____
_____
_____
_____

2. What are you currently doing to contribute to the success of your child?

_____
_____
_____
_____
_____

Chapter 18
The Widow at Zarephath

The widows' act of intercession was obeying Elijah's request.

Shana Wise

The Widow at Zarephath

Then the word of the Lord came to him:

"Go at once to Zarephath in the region of Sidon and stay there. I have directed a widow there to supply you with food." So he went to Zarephath. When he came to the town gate, a widow was there gathering sticks. He called to her and asked, "Would you bring me a little water in a jar so I may have a drink?" As she was going to get it, he called, "And bring me, please, a piece of bread."

"As surely as the Lord your God lives," she replied, "I don't have any bread—only a handful of flour in a jar and a little olive oil in a jug. I am gathering a few sticks to take home and make a meal for myself and my son, that we may eat it—and die."

Elijah said to her, "Don't be afraid. Go home and do as you have said. But first make a small loaf of bread for me from what you have and bring it to me, and then make something for yourself and your son. For this is what the Lord, the God of Israel, says: 'The jar of flour will not be used up and the jug of oil will not run dry until the day the Lord sends rain on the land.'"

She went away and did as Elijah had told her. So there was food every day for Elijah and for the woman and her family. For the jar of flour was not used up and the jug of oil did not run dry, in keeping with the word of the Lord spoken by Elijah (1 Kings 17:8-16).

Acts of Intercession

This story does not give the name of the widow at Zarephath, however it does paint a picture of the type of woman she was. She was a widow, she was poor, and she was a mother. During this time there was a severe drought and famine in the land (due to Israel's disobedience to God).

One day she went to go gather sticks for her and her son's last meal. She met a man named Elijah. He asked her to do something illogical; he requested that she feed him the first portion of her and her son's last meal. Her response to this request would seal the fate of her and her son.

In our lives, we will have to do things that we do not feel like doing. We have busy schedules, deadlines to meet, family gatherings, business meetings, church functions, children's sports, etc. We often have a hard time balancing these different areas of our lives because we have not disciplined ourselves with the Word, or we have a hard time prioritizing what needs to be done. We do not manage our time to benefit us. Sometimes we just have too much on our plates.

There will be times where we will be asked to do something that does not quite fit with our program. At that place, we find ourselves getting into a tug of war between flesh, feelings, and the spirit.

For example, you may be running late for work, because you wanted to sleep in extra ten minutes. On top of that you forgot to grab your lunch and you only have five dollars in your pocket. On your way to work you see someone holding a sign saying that they are hungry, out of work, and they need a dollar. Your eyes connect with that person and you see the hunger in their eyes. What do you do? Do you give them your last five dollars and be late for work and go without lunch? Or do you keep going and say to yourself, "I will pray for them to be blessed by someone else."

Or, for some reason an unforeseen financial circumstance comes about. You are living pay-check-to-pay-check. Payday comes and the thought comes to your mind, "If I pay my tithes, how am I going to make it for the next two weeks? Do I pay God or do I wait until I get into a better situation?"

Or, Wednesday night arrives and you have been working a 40-plus hour a week. It is 5 p.m., you are tired, had a long day at work, and all you want to do is stay at home and RE-LAX. Then you ask yourself, "Do I want to stay home or go to church?"

Romans 7:21-23 states: *I find then a law, that when I would do good, evil is present with me. For I delight in the law of God after the inward man: But I see another law of my members, warring against the law of my mind, and bringing me into captivity to the law of sin, which is my members.*

There is always war going on in our bodies between the flesh and the law—which is the Word of God. We need to obey God despite of our feelings, situations and circumstances. Our availability can determine the outcome of our blessings. We need to position ourselves to receive a blessing.

Elijah was a prophet of God. In the first book of Kings, Elijah had declared a drought in the land. He had just left the brook of Cherith and was on his way to Zarephath, as the Lord commanded. There was a widow woman at the gate of the city, gathering sticks. She was gathering sticks to go and cook her perceived last meal. What intrigued me about this woman in the text is that she knew that the situation that she was facing was not hopeful, yet she continued to do her daily function.

Many questions went through my head like:

What if she decided to stay home and be depressed because this was her last meal?

What if she did not feel like going to get the sticks because she was tired and or sick?

What if she did not want to go because she did not want people to see her in her despair?

This widow woman was steadfast in her position as mother and homemaker despite the fact she and her family were facing death by starvation. Just by showing up at the gate to gather sticks, she made herself available; unaware she was about to receive a blessing.

We sometimes miss out on our blessing simply because we are not available to serve. We get caught up in our feelings or circumstances more than our faith. You may be going through something in your marriage, on your job, school, a financial situation, a bad doctor report, etc. During those difficult times, you need to assemble with the people of God, pray, and obey His Word; the answer and blessing is waiting in the Word of God.

We need to receive instruction for our blessings. The definition of a gate is a passageway. It is a place that can be closed or opened. The widow had been at this place many times but that day was different. On that day, the gate of heaven was going to be opened up to her. The opening of the gate was depending on if she was able to follow instructions from the man of God. Church is a gateway to God.

We come to church week after week and the Word is going forth. We can choose to close the gate by not obeying the word, or open the gate by obeying. Elijah was a prophet– God's spokesman. He was a divinely called minister who announced the Will of God to His people. He asked the woman to go and bring him something to drink and eat.

There will be a time in our lives where we will be asked to do something that will seem almost impossible for us to do on our own. Yet we must remember the words that Jesus spoke, "with man it is impossible, but with God all things are possible."

In verses 12-14, Elijah and the widow had a conversation. She told him about her circumstance. She told him that her and her son was about to eat their last meal and die. She spoke out of the fear of her hopelessness. Yet praise God that she told her business to the right person!

In life we are going to go through some trials and tribulations and we need to take them straight to God. Elijah was a representation of God. We need to cast our cares upon Jesus because he cares for us! Elijah told her not to fear and do what he asked—give him some cake first and then make some for her and her son. He gave her specific instructions.

God gives us specific instructions as well through His Word

and the Holy Ghost. We must follow them exactly how He gives them. If He says forgive...we must forgive. If He said tithe...we must tithed. If he says pray always...we must pray.

The Bible declares that, man ought not to live by bread alone, but by every Word that proceeds out of the mouth of God. The Bible also declares that He will give those pastors after His own heart that will feed them with knowledge and understanding. When we come to church we must not just listen to the Word of God, but obey it to the point of application as the widow did.

We must sustain our blessings. The widow followed the instructions exactly how they were given. Through her obedience, Elijah, her and her son ate for over a year! Her one act of faith overflowed to the prophet and the family. When we obey God, we are able to receive a blessing and be a blessing to someone else.

In this widow case, her obedience was a matter of life and death. Her family's life was dependent on her obedience. She received a Deuteronomy 28:1-14 blessing! She hearkened the voice of the Lord. We need to learn from this woman that no matter what, we need to be available to serve and follow instructions from God.

This woman chose to obey Elijah's request according to the word spoken from his mouth. The word was a direct message from God to her household. The word came with a promise that her needs would be met until the rain comes. She chose to believe the word spoken by the man of God and because of it she was blessed.

Application, Thoughts & Questions

Application
Will you obey today? Will you position yourself to receive your blessing?

Thought
How many times do we continue with our daily functions despite the circumstances? When we are discouraged are we still available to serve? Do we stay at home and focus on our problems or do we still go to church to hear a word?

Questions
1. Have you ever experience a situation like that of the widow's? What was your response? What was the outcome?

_____
_____
_____
_____
_____

2. What specific instructions have God given you as it relates to your purpose?

_____
_____
_____
_____
_____

Chapter 19
Poor Widow

The act of intercession by the widow was paying off her family's debt.

Shana Wise

Poor Widow

The wife of a man from the company of the prophets cried out to Elisha, "Your servant my husband is dead, and you know that he revered the Lord. But now his creditor is coming to take my two boys as his slaves."

Elisha replied to her, "How can I help you? Tell me, what do you have in your house?"

"Your servant has nothing there at all," she said, "except a small jar of olive oil."

Elisha said, "Go around and ask all your neighbors for empty jars. Don't ask for just a few. Then go inside and shut the door behind you and your sons. Pour oil into all the jars, and as each is filled, put it to one side."

She left him and shut the door behind her and her sons. They brought the jars to her and she kept pouring. When all the jars were full, she said to her son, "Bring me another one." But he replied, "There is not a jar left." Then the oil stopped flowing.

She went and told the man of God, and he said, "Go, sell the oil and pay your debts. You and your sons can live on what is left" (2 Kings 4:1-7).

Acts of Intercession

When the widow was faced with her sons being sold to slavery because of her dead husband's debt, she went to the man her husband had been studying under, the prophet, Elisha.
It is always difficult when your spouse dies, but what is more straining is when they die and leave you in debt. Sometimes individuals find themselves in this position because of poor planning (little or no life insurance), no savings account, and poor money management. In the widow's case, her husband's debts were so great that her sons were facing slavery.

Slavery was abolished in the United States, but many Americans are "slaves" to debt. Debt can hinder you from reaching your full potential because when you are trying to move forward, the debt is pulling you back. God's plan for us is to always be debt free, but because of various circumstances, that is not a way of life for many people.

The widow woman had a choice about how she was going to handle her debt. She could have just let her sons go and become slaves or she could do something about it. She chose to go to Elisha for help. Elisha was not only a prophet in Israel; he was also her husband's mentor. The widow had to know that Elisha was able to perform miracles and give good instruction.

The widow was facing a problem that she had no solution for, so she went to someone who could help her find a solution. She went to Elisha with anticipation of an answer for her problem. We can learn from her actions, when we face problems that are greater than our ability and resources, we need to go to someone with knowledge and expertise to help us.

What is important to note is that Elisha gave her specific instructions on how to become free of debt. The woman went immediately and did exactly what he told her to do. When someone gives us a word of knowledge through instruction, we must do it without hesitation and without error. She did what she was told and she got results.

The Word of God works in the same manner as well. There are many instructions in the book of the law and we need to obey them for positive results in our lives. God also places pastors, leaders, mentors, teachers, and various other people within and outside the church to help guide us in the direction we need to go to achieve our goals. Elisha was a man of God whose words could be trusted and also get results.

The woman needed Elisha to help her situation through his gifting of wisdom. Her sons needed her obedience of following the instruction given for their freedom. Her sons needed to help their mother execute the instruction given for the blessing. Everyone had to play their part and/or supply each other's need.

Why did Elisha tell the woman to "shut the door behind her?" Everyone does not need to know what you are going through. The woman was working on her blessing. Everyone did not need to see what God had for her to do. They may not have understood what was going on, and they may have tried to talk her out of it.

They also may have tried to use the method she was using for their own problems. They may have also told her to give the jars back they had gave her because they would have not wanted to see her getting blessed with their stuff. Whatever the case maybe be, Elisha had her to close the door, because this blessing was for her family only. God may have you to "shut the door" to what you are doing to receive your blessing. God may give you tailor-made instructions on how to solve your problems and it is not for everyone to know.

He gave her specific instructions and she followed them exactly. Once all the jars were filled, she went back to Elisha and asked him what to do with them. He told her to go and sell the oil, pay off your debts, and live off what you have left.

The woman and her sons did exactly what Elisha told them to do and it created an overflow of blessings. They had enough to pay off the debt and resources left over to live on. The overflow of their blessing was a sign that God performed the miracle through them. The overflow was a testimony to the blessing.

Application, Thoughts & Questions

Application
God places various gifts within all of us to help one another.

From whom the whole body fitly joined together and compacted by that which every joint supplieth, according to the effectual working in the measure of every part, maketh increase of the body unto the edifying of itself in love (Ephesians 4:16).

Is there someone in your life you can go to for help in a time of need? If not, pray for God to lead that person into your life.

Questions

1. Do you own debt? Has it overwhelmed you? How?

_____
_____
_____
_____
_____

2. What are you currently doing to get out of debt?

_____
_____
_____
_____
_____

4. What is your spiritual gift? How are you using it to help others? If you do not know it, pray for revelation.

Chapter 20
Woman of Shunem

The act of intercession by the Shunammite woman was her finding Elisha in her son's time of need.

Woman of Shunem

Then Elisha said, "Call her." So he called her, and she stood in the doorway. "About this time next year," Elisha said, "you will hold a son in your arms."

"No, my lord!" she objected. "Please, man of God, don't mislead your servant!" But the woman became pregnant, and the next year about that same time she gave birth to a son, just as Elisha had told her.

The child grew, and one day he went out to his father, who was with the reapers. He said to his father, "My head! My head! His father told a servant, "Carry him to his mother."

After the servant had lifted him up and carried him to his mother, the boy sat on her lap until noon, and then he died. She went up and laid him on the bed of the man of God, then shut the door and went out.

When she reached the man of God at the mountain, she took hold of his feet. Gehazi came over to push her away, but the man of God said, "Leave her alone! She is in bitter distress, but the Lord has hidden it from me and has not told me why."

"Did I ask you for a son, my lord?" she said. "Didn't I tell you 'Don't raise my hopes'?"

Elisha said to Gehazi, "Tuck your cloak into your belt, take my staff in your hand and run. Don't greet anyone you meet, and if anyone greets you, do not answer. Lay my staff on the boy's face."

Acts of Intercession

But the child's mother said, "As surely as the Lord lives and as you live, I will not leave you." So he got up and followed her.

He went in, shut the door on the two of them and prayed to the Lord. Then he got on the bed and lay on the boy, mouth to mouth, eyes to eyes, hands to hands. As he stretched himself out on him, the boy's body grew warm. Elisha turned away and walked back and forth in the room and then got on the bed and stretched out on him once more. The boy sneezed seven times and opened his eyes.

Elisha summoned Gehazi and said, "Call the Shunammite." And he did. When she came, he said, "Take your son." She came in, fell at his feet and bowed to the ground. Then she took her son and went out (2 Kings 4:15-21, 27-30, 33-37).

The story of the Shunammite woman is a story of a relationship between her (and her family) and the prophet, Elisha. She reverenced him as the man of God and she help aid him with some of the physical needs of his ministry for she and her husband were wealthy. Whenever Elisha came to town, she provided him with food to eat. She and her husband agreed to build him a room on the upper level of their home, so when he was came to town he had a place to stay. The room had a bed, table, chair, and lamp–all provided to care for the need of the prophet.

The woman of Shunammite lifestyle reflected the principles of reaping and sowing. She and her husband were wealthy and she wanted to sow into Elisha's ministry. Their home was made into a lodging for Elisha when he was ministering in town. Through Elisha's ministry, he was able to meet the spiritual needs of people, through this woman's wealth.

She was helping to meet Elisha's physical needs with food, shelter, and a resting place. She went above and beyond to make him feel welcomed in her home by building an upstairs room just for him. The significance of him having a room was to provide him privacy without distraction. Elisha's ministry consisted of performing miracles, teaching, and giving messages to Israel.

The woman's house was a place for rest and rejuvenation for Elisha, which would have been much needed because of the amount of ministry he was doing on a daily basis. Due to her generosity towards the prophet he wanted to bless her. He told her that she would have a child within a year despite the fact that she was barren. At first she did not believe it, but she conceived and had a son.

When you bless others, blessings will come back to you. Elisha's spoken blessing over the woman was a blessing that she did not ask for. She had accepted the fact that she would never be a mother, yet she still chose to be a blessing to someone else. She used her wealth to aid in the ministry of Elisha and in return she received a blessing money could not buy.

Wealth can cause people to become inwardly focused if they let money be the center of their life. Also, it can make you waste money on things that you do not need because you are trying to fill an empty void in your life. There is nothing wrong with being wealthy; the problem lies where wealth/money becomes your god.

The woman gave to the man of God out of the abundance of her heart through money. Money is a tool used to get things accomplished in earth but it is not the answer to every problem. The woman had a condition of infertility that she had adapted to as a way of life for her and her husband. Little did she know that the birth of her child would be activated by her hospitality toward Elisha.

Many of our blessings are connected to other people. There is a saying that, "you are one person away from your blessing." God's kingdom operates on the principle, "you are blessed to be a blessing to others." Elisha's ministry consisted of speaking a repented word unto the nation of Israel (they had turned from God), blessing others in need through miracles, and teaching other prophets. He touched, blessed many lives in a positive manner through his ministry. In return, God provided his physical needs through this woman's hospitality. Through the birth of the child, the woman and her husband were able to have an heir to their wealth.

Just like the woman of Shunammite, we can choose to be a blessing to others as well. You do not have to be wealthy to bless someone else; you just have to be willing. A willing heart is what God desires. He blesses us every day of our lives because He loves us. Our love for God should be the fuel for us to bless others. Giving does not always have to be monetary; it can come through various other ways such as spiritual, emotional, and physical.

Remember, the woman received a blessing that money could not buy. It was a spoken word through Elisha that manifested in her life. Our words have the power to bless others in a way that can change their life forever. The widow participated in her miracle blessing. Her child had an episode while he was working in the field with his father that caused him to become sick and die. When the child was brought home to his mother, she took him up and laid him on Elisha's bed.

Her history with Elisha and his spoken word of prophecy fulfilled in her life through her child sparked her to move on faith. Just by her laying her child on his bed signified that she was not accepting her son's untimely death as the final end. This was the first step the woman took toward working on the behalf of her son's resurrection.

She left the house and went to find Elisha to tell him what happened to her son. When she arrived where he was, she insisted that Elisha come to the house. She wanted the man who spoke life over her to be the one to bring him back from the dead. This woman had bold faith in Elisha and her determination and trust in this man of God helped bring forth the miracle. When Elisha arrived, he was able to restore life back to her son.

When we work our faith through the word of God, He is able to make things happen for us that we could not do on our own. The Webster's Dictionary definition of a miracle is an extraordinary event manifesting divine intervention in human affairs. Miracles happen to individuals who are willing to participate.

Elisha the prophet is not available to us today (he was a representative of God during this period of time) but we do have access to the Father through His son Jesus Christ. God is able to work miracles on our behalf, but sometimes we need to do like the woman did and work our faith. She was a giver, she believed in God's prophet, and she was determined that the man of God was able to bring her son back to life.

But it wasn't over. She also receives another blessing for her obedience. Now Elisha had said to the woman whose son he had restored to life, "Go away with your family and stay for a while wherever you can, because the Lord has decreed a famine in the land that will last seven years." The woman proceeded to do as the man of God said. She and her family went away and stayed in the land of the Philistines seven years. At the end of the seven years she came back from the land of the Philistines and went to appeal to the king for her house and land.

The king was talking to Gehazi, the servant of the man of God, and had said, "Tell me about all the great things Elisha has done." Just as Gehazi was telling the king how Elisha had restored the dead to life, the woman whose son Elisha had brought back to life came to appeal to the king for her house and land.

Gehazi said, "This is the woman, my lord the king, and this is her son whom Elisha restored to life." The king asked the woman about it, and she told him. Then he assigned an official to her case and said to him, "Give back everything that belonged to her, including all the income from her land from the day she left the country until now" (2 Kings 8:1-6).

Isn't it amazing how God orchestrates divine connection with timing? The woman of Shunem and her son arrived just as Gehazi and the king were talking about the miracle Elisha performed in their lives. (They had just arrived back from that land of Philistine were they had been living for seven years because of the famine in the land Elisha had warned them about.)

Shana Wise

Her son's life was a living testimony of what God had performed through Elisha. Just by the king witnessing the young man and his mother, it caused him to restore everything they left behind before the famine, including the income that was made from her land.

We have to remember that this woman was wealthy before she left and wealth was restored to her when she came back. What a blessing! The Bible states, "you reap what you sow." The woman sowed into Elisha's ministry for many years and because of it she was blessed.

We can do the same thing the woman did by sowing into the Kingdom of God. Remember that our giving is connected to someone else's life. When we tithed and bring our offering unto God, we are helping to establish His Kingdom on earth. We must make sure that we are giving our money and resources to the people, places, and things that God has for us to give to.

He will instruct you where and how to give. It may be in a church setting, non-profit organization, or to an individual He has placed in your life. Just make sure that you are doing it from your heart and out of your obedience to God.

Elisha did not have to ask the woman to give to him; she did it on her own will, and that's how it should be for us. Give because you see a need. Give out of your love for God and His people. The woman was blessed for her continual faithfulness and because of it she had favor with God and man. This favor caused a blessing to come without her having to ask for them-they just followed her.

Application, Thoughts & Questions

Thought

Now unto him that is able to do exceeding abundantly above all that we ask or think, according to the power that worketh in us (Ephesians 3:20).

This scripture reminds us that God is able to do the impossible through the possible effort that we put forth. The woman worked her miracle for her son and because of it he lived.

Questions

1. How is your home environment? Is it a sanctuary for rest, relaxation and rejuvenation? How is your hospitality to guest?

_____

_____

_____

_____

_____

2. How are you using your resources to bless others? Who has blessed you with their resources?

_____

_____

_____

_____

_____

3. What miracles have you experienced or witnessed in your life?

_____

_____

_____

_____

_____

4. You may have some seemingly "dead situations" in your life (lost dreams, low income, bad marriage, etc.) but are you willing to trust God to day for your miracle? Are you willing to participate in your blessing?

If so, what is God having you do? How are you praying and obeying His Word?

_____

_____

_____

_____

_____

5. Do you have a testimony of how you have been faithful to God over a long period of time, and in return received His blessing? What extraordinary blessing was tailor made for you?

_____

_____

_____

_____

_____

Reflect on the blessings and favor over your life.

Chapter 21
Jehosheba

Jehosheba's act of intercession was preventing Joash from being killed so he could fulfill his destiny of being king of Judah.

Jehosheba

When Athaliah the mother of Ahaziah saw that her son was dead, she proceeded to destroy the whole royal family. But Jehosheba, the daughter of King Jehoram and sister of Ahaziah, took Joash son of Ahaziah and stole him away from among the royal princes, who were about to be murdered.

She put him and his nurse in a bedroom to hide him from Athaliah; so he was not killed. He remained hidden with his nurse at the temple of the Lord for six years while Athaliah ruled the land (2 Kings 11:1-3).

During this period in Israel's history–specifically in the land of Judah's southern kingdom, the nation was ruled by Queen Athaliah. She was a wicked idol worshipper who came to power after the murder of her son, King Ahaziah. She wanted to kill all remaining members of the royal family to secure the throne for her. She was willing to kill her own family members to become the leader of Israel.

Idol worship during the time of this story consisted of worshipping everything but the True and Living God. Some examples of public idol worshipping during this period were human sacrifices (including sacrificing children), elicit sex within the idol temple, worship of others gods such as Baal and Ashtoreth. Idol worship practiced by an individual, families and nation brought corruption, dysfunction and eventually destruction.

Jehosheba was married to a priest who served in the temple of God, and they lived differently than her brother and his family. She was the sister of the late King Ahaziah and she was married to Jehoiada who was a priest in the temple of God. Her nephew, Joash was king Ahaziah's son. Joash was next in line for the throne but, he was just a baby.

Jehosheba hid him and his nurse in the temple of the Lord for six years. The temple of the Lord was a great place to hide her nephew because queen Athaliah worshipped idol gods, not the true and living God; therefore she would not go into His temple. There were two significant reasons Joash's life was important to the nation of Israel:

1. This story takes place in a period when Judah had been lead by leaders (Kings Jehoram, Ahaziah, and Queen Athaliah) who worshipped idol gods. It was time for a king to lead Judah back to worshipping God. Joash would be that leader. He was literally raised in the temple of God and by the priest Jehoiada.

2. Joash's bloodline consisted of a family of idol worshippers, but they were all still descendants of King David, and in the lineage of Christ. Joash's life and rule over Israel was part of prophecy being fulfilled in the Old and New Testaments. God made a promise to David that his descendants would rule the throne of Israel.

When God made this promise to King David, he had to fulfill it. Even though the idol worshipping royalty that ruled Israel were unfaithful to God, He has always been faithful to His word. God would not allow His people to suffer under idol worshipping leaders forever. He would use king Joash to bring His people them back to worshipping Him.

Children are a gift from God, and it is our responsibility as parents to teach them right from wrong. We are living in a time when children are not receiving those principles from their parents. Joash would have learned their ways of idol worship, and he would have continued to lead Israel into idol worship had he been raised by his father and grand-mother. Jehosheba and her husband taught Joash right from wrong. They taught him to follow the law of God.

Dysfunction, idol worshipping, and bad parenting are a way of life for many individuals and families today. There is a movement going on in the world today that centers on idol-ization, political correctness, and selfishness. Pornography, "star watching" (paparazzi updating the world on what celebrities are doing), image mutation, drugs, illicit sex, idol music, idol television, social media and other outlets, are having more influence on our children and adults than the word of God.

We may have family members who practice these types of behaviors in their lives. As believers, our job is to use our God given influence to hold up a standard of righteousness within the family. Jehosheba and her husband were a great example of what this looks like. In spite of the wickedness their family chose to do, they chose to live their lives righ-teously. She saved her nephew's life from being taken by his grandmother.

We can aid in saving someone else's life by teaching them the ways of God through our lifestyle. They may not come and live with us, but our influence in their life can help shape their future. Jehosheba's action of saving her nephew's life and raising him as one of her own, helped shape his future as the next king of Israel.

She and her husband Jehoiada, raised him to worship the true and living God. And because of this rearing, Joash was able to rule Israel righteously in the way of the Lord. His top priority during his reign was to make repairs to the Lord's temple. He wanted the people to come and bring their sacrifices to God, not to the pagan shrines they were previously accustom to worshipping. He wanted to restore the order of worship as God had originally designed it.

Application, Thoughts & Questions

Questions

1. Joash was destined to be king and Jehosheba and her husband helped him to fulfill his destiny.

Who has God placed in your life to help fulfill their destiny?

_____

_____

_____

_____

_____

Write the names of the people in your family who need God in their lives. Pray for them on a regular basis. Ask God what He has for you to do in their lives.

_____

_____

_____

_____

_____

Chapter 22
Huldah

Huldah's act of intercession was confirming the Word from the Lord.

ℋuldah

Hilkiah the high priest said to Shaphan the secretary, "I have found the Book of the Law in the temple of the Lord."

He gave it to Shaphan, who read it. Then Shaphan the secretary went to the king and reported to him: "Your officials have paid out the money that was in the temple of the Lord and have entrusted it to the workers and supervisors at the temple."

Then Shaphan the secretary informed the king, "Hilkiah the priest has given me a book." And Shaphan read from it in the presence of the king.

When the king heard the words of the Book of the Law, he tore his robes. He gave these orders to Hilkiah the priest, Ahikam son of Shaphan, Akbor son of Micaiah, Shaphan the secretary and Asaiah the king's attendant: "Go and inquire of the Lord for me and for the people and for all Judah about what is written in this book that has been found. Great is the Lord's anger that burns against us because those who have gone before us have not obeyed the words of this book; they have not acted in accordance with all that is written there concerning us."

Hilkiah the priest, Ahikam, Akbor, Shaphan and Asaiah went to speak to the prophet Huldah, who was the wife of Shallum son of Tikvah, the son of Harhas, keeper of the wardrobe. She lived in Jerusalem, in the New Quarter.

She said to them, "This is what the Lord, the God of Israel, says: Tell the man who sent you to me, 'This is what the Lord says: I am going to bring disaster on this place and its people, according to everything written in the book the king of Judah has read. Because they have forsaken me and burned incense to other gods and aroused my anger by all the idols their hands have made, my anger will burn against this place and will not be quenched.'

"Tell the king of Judah, who sent you to inquire of the Lord, 'This is what the Lord, the God of Israel, says concerning the words you heard: Because your heart was responsive and you humbled yourself before the Lord when you heard what I have spoken against this place and its people—that they would become a curse and be laid waste—and because you tore your robes and wept in my presence, I also have heard you, declares the Lord. Therefore I will gather you to your ancestors, and you will be buried in peace. Your eyes will not see all the disaster I am going to bring on this place.'" So they took her answer back to the king. (2 Kings 22:8-20).

King Josiah was in power and he wanted to bring the people back to worshipping God. He instituted reforms to restore the temple of God. Hilkiah, the high priest, had just found the book of the law in the temple (the book became lost in the temple because the nation of Israel had been ruled by kings who worshipped idol gods up until this point).

Staphan took the scroll (book of the law) to King Josiah and read it to him. The word stated that God was going to bring judgment upon Judah because they have not kept the commandments.

This made King Josiah very sad and he outwardly expressed his humility through the tearing of his clothes. He sent Staphan to go and find out more information about what they just read. The priest and others in the temple went to prophet Huldah to tell her about what had just happened. She confirmed that what they read was going to come to pass in Judah; she stated that the judgment would happen after King Josiah died.

There are two lessons to be learned from this passage:

1. If we do not understand the Word of God we need to go to someone who can help. Receiving knowledge and under-standing of the Word will help us move forward and grow in God. There is a saying, "when you know better, do better." That is true regarding your growth in God.

Huldah was able to make them understand why the judg-ment was about to happen and when it would take place (after King Josiah died). This shared information was help-ful because they were in the process of restoring the temple. King Josiah and the workers in the temple needed to know the importance of worshipping God and the consequences that come when you do not. When we go to church, it is the pastor's responsibility to feed the congregation with knowl-edge and understanding (Jer.3:15).

2. Huldah had to speak the truth about the Word even though it was not good news for Judah's future. We need to speak the truth about God's Word as well. Some people like to be surrounded by those who only tell them what they want to hear. This is dangerous because it will stunt their growth and hinder their progress. When someone is doing wrong or heading in the wrong direction, we need to be able to speak the truth to them in love. God's Word is truth and love.
Love does not always feel good, but it is good for us. For example, a parent will discipline their child when they are

doing wrong; they do this because they love them. They do not want their child to grow up unruly and lawless because they know that it will lead to disaster. It is the same with God; he wants the best for us and that's why he has given us His Word. His Word is the truth given in love. As we grow in God's word he will teach us how to confront evil with the truth.

Huldah was a prophet in Israel. The priest and others in the temple had respect for her words of wisdom. Since the book of the law was lost for many years, the priests were not able to study it on a regular basis. So when they received the word, it was probably hard for them to understand or interpret it correctly. Huldah's anointing of prophecy enabled her to confirm the word that was read.

Application, Thoughts & Questions

Application

Are you connected to a Bible-teaching church where you are growing in the Word of God? If you are not receiving it, then pray to God about where you need to be.

Questions

1. Are you comfortable confronting people with, or speaking the truth? If not, why?

_____
_____
_____
_____
_____

2. How has God's word confronted the sin in your life?

_____
_____
_____
_____
_____

Chapter 23
Esther

**Esther's act of intercession was
risking her life to save her people.**

Esther

"Go, gather together all the Jews who are in Susa, and fast for me. Do not eat or drink for three days, night or day. I and my attendants will fast as you do. When this is done, I will go to the king, even though it is against the law. And if I perish, I perish" (Esther 4:16).

The book of Esther takes place in the land of Persia. The Jewish people were the minority living there and many people hated them because of their race. Esther was a beautiful Jewish woman who was married to King Xerxes. Esther was more than just beautiful on the outside; her beauty came from within and was priceless. Her willingness to risk her life for her people was something to behold and admire. Many women today use their looks for their own personal gain and agenda. Esther used her influence with King Xerxes to bring social change and justice.

She was more than just a pretty face. She was smart, brave, courageous and compassionate. In the world we live in today, vanity is ruling the lives of many women more than God's Word. Everything that God creates is beautiful to Him, yet the world continues to define beauty. The world's definition of beauty can be superficial and deceiving. Young girls are shaped by what the culture dictates as beauty.

Esther is a great role model to the women of the world today because she was able to show that her (influential) physical beauty was used as an avenue to represent the God she served.

Acts of Intercession

Her cousin, Mordecai was a high official in the government who had a rivalry with another high official in the government named, Haman. Haman was an evil man who hated the Jews and wanted them exterminated because Mordecai refused to bow down and worship him. Through his deception he persuaded the King to issue an order of assassination of all the Jews. When Mordecai got word of Haman's evil intentions he informed Esther. She had her people (within the palace and in Susa) fast and pray with and for her before she went to speak with the king.

There are going to be difficult decisions and challenging times in life, and some of those times are going to call for prayer and fasting. Prayer and fasting helps us tap into the supernatural place that we need to be for divine strength and guidance. Fasting requires one to deny themselves of food or any other distraction. Denying ourselves of what we want, helps to aid in the process of receiving what God has for us.

Esther had a specific purpose for fasting; it was a matter of life and death! Instead of doing nothing, Esther decided to risk her life by going to see the king. It was against the law to be in the king's presence without invitation, and the penalty for breaking the law was death. However, the king was pleased to see her and he asked what she wanted.

She requested that the king and Haman come to a banquet she had prepared for them. They came to the banquet and then attended another one after that. The king asked Esther what she wanted; stating she could have anything. He even proposed giving her half of his kingdom. Instead of thinking about her own personal gain, she took the opportunity and advocated for her people that were about to be destroyed.

She made the king aware of the conspiracy that was taking place as it related to Haman and his intentions for her people.

Because of this bold move on Esther's behalf, her people were saved from death. The result of the fast was life changing—for her people, Haman, King Xerxes, Modecai, and the whole nation of Persia. Haman and his family lost their lives due to Haman's plot to kill innocent people. Modecai was promoted to a higher position within the kingdom. King Xerxes instituted laws to empower the Jews in their defense.

Prayer and fasting gets results. And, our selfless acts can bring life to other people. Self-centeredness is the way of the world today. Many of the distractions we face on a daily basis have to do with our inward desires and most times they have nothing to do with growing the kingdom of God. These distractions keep us focused on getting our needs met rather than meeting the needs of others.

The God we serve is always thinking about us. His act of sending His son to die for us was a selfless act that brings life to everyone who accepts him. Esther was focused on the preservation of her people and she was prepared to die for them rather than to stay silent. We were sent here to earth to be a blessing to others and represent the kingdom of God on earth; unfortunately this is not taking place in our lives because we are so distracted.

Esther took the opportunity and revealed to the king about Haman's plot to kill the Jews. King Xerxes had Haman killed and the king retracted the order to have the Jews killed. He also instituted other laws to make life better for the Jews living in Persia.

Application, Thoughts & Questions

Questions

1. God made us all beautiful in His eyes. How are you using your beautiful God-given influence?

_____

_____

_____

_____

_____

2. What are some things detracting you from serving others?

_____

_____

_____

_____

_____

What things are you seeking God for in your life? Pray and fast on these things as the spirit of God leads you.

Acts of Intercession

Women of the New Testament

Chapter 24

Mary

Mother of Jesus

Mary's act of intercession was her response to the word given by the angel of the Lord.

Mary
Mother of Jesus

The angel answered, "The Holy Spirit will come on you, and the power of the Most High will overshadow you. So the holy one to be born will be called the Son of God. Even Elizabeth your relative is going to have a child in her old age, and she who was said to be unable to conceive is in her sixth month. For no word from God will ever fail."

"I am the Lord's servant," Mary answered. "May your word to me be fulfilled." Then the angel left her (Luke 1:35-38).

Mary was chosen to be the mother of Jesus. She was young, a virgin, and she was engaged to Joseph when she received the word from the angel of the Lord. Her response to the word spoke volumes. The word she spoke was a great foundation for the rest of the events (concerning her personal life, Jesus, and the church) that she would witness in her lifetime.

Mary chose to speak life when she received the message from the Lord. She stated that she is a servant of the Lord and that His word will be fulfilled in her life. She could have focused on her circumstances of not being married, being a virgin, what would people think, and she could have be killed because she was pregnant out wedlock; but she chose to serve God rather than her feelings.

We must chose life as well, but sometimes we chose death

because of our response to the word. Blatant disobedience to God's word can bring death to your purpose on earth. Every time we choose to respond the wrong way to God's Word, it hinders our growth in Him and our purpose on earth. When we choose to obey God's word blessings come to us.

Mary's blessing was that God worked on her behalf. She was not killed for being pregnant out of wedlock, and Joseph did marry her and raise Jesus as his son. She was able to witness Jesus grow into a man. She was able to witness wonderful things that Jesus did here on earth. Serving God is an honor and privilege that we all have access to, but many people would rather serve themselves rather than God.

The angel stated to Mary, "For no Word from God will ever fail." This statement is still true today. We may fail at various things in our life, but God never fails. When God speaks it is for keeps. God's Word will come to pass in our lives. God's Word contains everything we need to live a productive and fulfilled life.

The Bible is the instruction manual for us; we must read it to find out our purpose in Him. Failure does not exist in the Kingdom of God and since his Word will never fail us, we have victory in whatever we are going through. Mary trusted everything that the angel of the Lord spoke unto her, and the Word came to pass.

Trusting in God's Word brings forth growth inside you. Mary trusted the Word spoken to her and the Word began to grow inside her. She physically carried The Word inside of her. We spiritually carry the word through the Holy Ghost residing inside of us. Jesus Christ fulfilled prophecy through his ministry. God wants to fulfill things in our life through His Word, but we have to trust Him just like Mary did. We need to respond to His word through obedience.

We all have been chosen by God to do something for Him here on earth, it is called our purpose. Mary's purpose was to be the earthly mother of Jesus the Savior of the world. God chose a willing vessel to carry Jesus. Her response to the word was a reflection of her heart towards God. Her intention was to serve God according to His will in her life.

When our hearts are focused toward God, our response should reflect Mary's. She accepted God's Will for her life and so should we. God's Will for us to is to have life and have it more abundantly (John 10:10). Mary was not only just carrying life; she was carrying the one who would bring eternal life to everyone who would accept him. We also carry life inside of us as well.

We are God's children and we are a reflection of Him. In God there is life and we are His witnesses, physically and spiritually. Our purpose in God is to help bring life to others through our testimony of Jesus Christ in our lives.

Application, Thoughts & Questions

Thought
Your response to the Word of God can bless or curse you.

The tongue has the power of life and death and those who love it will eat its fruit (Proverbs 18:21).

Questions

1. How is God using you to bring life to others? If you cannot answer that question ask God to reveal His purpose for your life.

_____
_____
_____
_____
_____

Write out the areas in your life where you need to obey God more.

_____
_____
_____
_____
_____

2. What Word (scripture) do you trust God to do in your life that has not yet come to pass?

_____
_____
_____
_____
_____

Chapter 25
Elizabeth

Elizabeth's act of intercession was advocating for her son's name.

Elizabeth

When it was time for Elizabeth to have her baby, she gave birth to a son. Her neighbors and relatives heard that the Lord had shown her great mercy, and they shared her joy.
On the eighth day they came to circumcise the child, and they were going to name him after his father Zechariah, but his mother spoke up and said, "No! He is to be called John."

They said to her, "There is no one among your relatives who has that name."

Then they made signs to his father, to find out what he would like to name the child. He asked for a writing tablet, and to everyone's astonishment he wrote, "His name is John." Immediately his mouth was opened and his tongue set free, and he began to speak, praising God. All the neighbors were filled with awe, and throughout the hill country of Judea people were talking about all these things (Luke 1: 57-65).

Elizabeth and Zachariah were an older couple who had been married for many years without the ability to have children. The angel of the Lord appeared to Zachariah in the temple and told him that his wife was going to have a child. Zachariah questioned the angel out of disbelief. Because of his disbelief, he was literally "muted."

Shortly after this incident, Elizabeth became pregnant and gave birth to a son. Her neighbors and family members came by the house on the day of his circumcision and told Elizabeth to name him after his father. She quickly resisted their suggestion because they did not know what God had already told Zechariah and her to name him.

We have to be careful whom we let speak into our lives. Their intentions may be good, but good intentions do not always bring positive results. When God has given us specific instructions, we must obey them. What God has for you is for you and not everybody will understand what He is doing in your life. And, we have to remember what God has done for us already.

Zachariah's muteness was a constant reminder that he received a Word from the angel Gabriel, and that the Word was spoken from God. And it came to pass in his life. Elizabeth was able to experience the Holy Ghost coming upon her when she received a Word from her cousin, Mary in regards to her being chosen to carry Jesus. John leaped in her stomach when she was pregnant with him.

Just like Zachariah and Elizabeth we have to remember what God has specifically done in our lives that no one else knows about. We have to know who God is to us, personally. We have to know all the great and mighty things that He has done for us and the things that he has revealed to us through His word. When we know these things for ourselves, no one should be able to persuade us to do something out of the will of God.

The people at Zachariah's house wanted him to name his son after him. Zachariah could not speak at this point, but he could write. When he wrote that his son would be named John, immediately God opened his mouth and he was able to speak. God performed a miracle right in front of Zachariah's opposition. God will move on our behalf when we stand firm in His Word. He will cause others to witness His power through your belief and steadfastness in His word.

Zachariah also did not let his limitation of being speechless hinder him from standing up for God's Word. His wife Elizabeth was able to speak and advocate for John's name, but the people ignored her and requested Zachariah's opinion. He supported his wife's advocacy through the action he took by writing John's name. Elizabeth and Zachariah were a husband and wife on one accord as it related to the Will of God within their family unit. They would not let anyone come in their house and disrupt what God was doing in their lives.

Do not let the opinions of others override what God has already spoken to you. The angel of God (Gabriel) told Zachariah in the temple he was to name the baby, John. The people who had come to Zachariah's house did not know what God was doing in the lives of him and his wife.

They were not there when Gabriel spoke to Zachariah in the temple. They did not know that Zachariah was temporarily mute because he did not believe the Word spoken to him. They did not know the calling on John's life and that he leapt in his mother's womb when she received the word of the coming of the Lord. They did not know that it was God who enabled them to conceive John in their old age.

Lastly, they did not know that John's birth was activated by the future birth of Jesus Christ, the Savior of the world. John was chosen by God to be the prophet to prepare the people's heart for Christ's ministry.

Application, Thoughts & Questions

Question

1. Have people tried to get you to do things that you know God did not tell you to do? How did you respond and what was the outcome?

_____

_____

_____

_____

_____

Write down a list of things that God has spoken or revealed to you that no one else knows about.

Reflect on these things when opposition comes your way.

_____

_____

_____

_____

_____

_____

Chapter 26
Anna

Anna's act of intercession was testifying to everyone that she encountered Jesus Christ.

Anna

There was also a prophet, Anna, the daughter of Penuel, of the tribe of Asher. She was very old; she had lived with her husband seven years after her marriage, and then was a widow until she was eighty-four. She never left the temple but worshiped night and day, fasting and praying.

Coming up to them at that very moment, she gave thanks to God and spoke about the child to all who were looking forward to the redemption of Jerusalem. When Joseph and Mary had done every-thing required by the Law of the Lord, they returned to Galilee to their own town of Nazareth (Luke 2:36-39).

Anna was an elderly widow prophet who worshipped in the temple every day, fasting and praying. This was her routine for many years; she never left the temple. On this particular day all of her prayers were about to manifest right before her eyes. On this day Mary and Joseph had brought baby Jesus to the temple to make an offering for him according to the law.

Her response was to praise God and to witness to people about the child who had come to Jerusalem. She had been fasting and praying in the temple for years. The Bible does not even say what her prayers were about, but it does say that when she came up to Simeon, Joseph, Mary, and baby Jesus, she gave thanks to God and spoke about the child to all who were looking forward to the redemption of Jerusa-lem.

Her life was changed that day, and because of it, her routine changed from fasting and praying, to telling everyone she encountered in the temple about Jesus.

When we pray and fast we should be expecting God to answer us with a revelation of His Word. The root word of revelation is *reveal*. Anna's witnessing of baby Jesus Christ was God revealing her answer to what she had been praying and fasting about. Jesus is the answer to all of our petitions to God. God reveals the answer we need through His son Jesus.

In John 14:6, *Jesus saith unto him, I am the way, the truth, and the life: no man cometh unto the Father, but by me.* Jesus is the Word, and the revelation comes to us through the Word of God.

John 1:1-4 says, *In the beginning was the Word, and the Word was with God, and the Word was God. He was with God in the beginning. Through him all things were made; without him nothing was made that has been made. In him was life, and that life was the light of all mankind. The light shines in the darkness, and the darkness has not overcome it.*

Anna's prayer revelation is summed up in John 1:14:
The Word became flesh and made his dwelling among us. We have seen his glory, the glory of the one and only Son, who came from the Father, full of grace and truth.

There was a man named Simeon who had been waiting for the Messiah to come to Israel. He was a righteous man who was moved by the spirit of God to go to the temple that day. The Spirit had revealed to him that he would not die until we had seen the Savior of the world. When he saw baby Jesus he took him in his arms and started prophesying about Jesus.

He declared that he was the Savior. As he was prophesying, Anna came up and heard the words that Simeon was declaring about Jesus Christ. Immediately she started to praise God and tell all the people she encountered about Jesus who was the redeemer of Jerusalem.

Application, Thoughts & Questions

Application

God answered Anna in a great in mighty way. As we fast and pray expect God to answer. Reflect on these scriptures.

Now unto him that is able to do exceeding abundantly above all that we ask or think, according to the power that worketh in us (Ephesians 3:20 (KJV)).

Call unto me, and I will answer thee, and shew thee great and mighty things, which thou knowest not (Jeremiah 33:3 (KJV)).

Anna praised God when she received her answer. This outward expression of praise shows gratitude and reverence to the Almighty God. God answers our prayers so that we can be a blessing to others. Do not be ashamed to share your testimony of faith through Jesus Christ. Jesus also shared a parable to his disciples about how we should be persistent in our prayers.

Read the following: Luke 18:1-8 (NIV) and write how this text relates to Anna's story and what it means to you:

Then Jesus told his disciples a parable to show them that they should always pray and not give up. He said: "In a certain town there was a judge who neither feared God nor cared what people thought. And there was a widow in that town who kept coming to him with the plea, 'Grant me justice against my adversary.' "For some time he refused. But finally he said to himself, 'Even though I don't fear God or care what people think, yet because this widow keeps bothering me, I will see that she gets justice, so that she won't eventually come and attack me!'"

And the Lord said, "Listen to what the unjust judge says. And will not God bring about justice for his chosen ones, who cry out to him day and night? Will he keep putting them off? I tell you, he will see that they get justice, and quickly. However, when the Son of Man comes, will he find faith on the earth?"

_____

_____

_____

_____

_____

_____

Questions

1. What is your response to answered prayers?

_____

_____

_____

_____

_____

2. What things are you still waiting on God to reveal to you?

_____

_____

_____

_____

_____

_____

_____

_____

_____

_____

_____

3. How will you use your answer to be a witness for him?

_____

_____

_____

_____

_____

_____

_____

_____

_____

_____

_____

Chapter 27
The Samaritan Woman

**The Samaritan woman's act of intercession
was evangelizing to her town.**

The Samaritan Woman

Many of the Samaritans from that town believed in him because of the woman's testimony, "He told me everything I ever did." So when the Samaritans came to him, they urged him to stay with them, and he stayed two days. And because of his words many more became believers.

They said to the woman, "We no longer believe just because of what you said; now we have heard for ourselves, and we know that this man really is the Savior of the world" (John 4:39-42).

The Samaritan woman was living a lifestyle of carnal worship and sexual immorality before she met Jesus. She met Jesus at the well in the middle of the day, which was unusual because the women of the town drew water during the morning hours. Her being there during noontime signified her living as an outcast in society because of her alternative lifestyle.

She had issues she struggled with internally and externally. Her lack of true worship internally was reflected in the poor decisions she made with men externally. She was living with a man who was not her husband and Jesus stated she had five husbands before him. Due to her lifestyle, the town's people looked at her as an outcast. She was shocked that Jesus was even holding a conversation with her because men were not supposed to talk to women in public places.

She also was a Samaritan, and many Jews thought that they were better than Samaritans (which in our day we call it racist or prejudice). She had a form of godliness but her view of God was narrowed down to worshipping Him on a mountain. With these internal and external issues going on, it did not stop the divine intervention that God had tailor-made for her.

Her encounter with Jesus brought forth an inward change of her view and worship of God that reciprocally changed her behavior externally. Her focus had changed from being consumed with her issues of carnality to being restored to the woman God created her to be. All of us have been created to worship God but because of sin in our lives, our worship becomes distorted and/or nonexistent. God's intervention of restoration will always impact our worship experience with Him.

Yet a time is coming and has now come when the true worshipers will worship the Father in the Spirit and in truth, for they are the kind of worshipers the Father seeks. 24 God is spirit, and his worshipers must worship in the Spirit and in truth
(John 4: 23-24 (NIV)).

God loves us and he wants us to enjoy the fullness of life that He has for us. He does not judge us like the world. He does not continually throw our past up in our face. Instead, His love for us overshadows the sin in our lives. He has designed our worship toward him to bring forth repentance and restoration. When repentance and restoration happens, God is able to use our testimony to get the glory.

God moved on the Samaritan woman's heart. Her heart was

previously filled with the burden of living a sinful life. Now her heart was filled with joy and praise. God brought the Samaritan woman out of darkness into His marvelous light, and the light caused her to have an overflow in her heart. She had a deep urgency to go and tell the people in her community about what she had just experienced. She knew that they needed Jesus just as she had.

Due to her strong and powerful testimony of how Jesus changed her life, many people thought that if he could do it for her, he could do it for them. Jesus did just that. He came and spent two days in the town and many people believed in him.

God can use anybody. He wants to use our testimony to draw people to him. The Samaritan woman's story gives other women who are not living a life pleasing to God, hope. It shows that our sin is not greater than His love for us. He has a tailor-made intervention waiting on you, and his name is Jesus Christ. When you accept Jesus as your Lord and Savior it will cause your life to change for the better. God wants to use everything that you have been through in your life—good or bad—and make it work for your good (Romans 8:28).

Her lifestyle did not stop Jesus from holding a conversation with her. He confronted her current living situation and her view of worshipping God (John 4:4-26). When the conversation ended, she realized she was not just talking to any man, she had been talking with Jesus the Christ. Her life was instantly changed. His words impacted her so much that she told the town's people about him and many others people were able to experience the same.

Application, Thoughts & Questions

Application

If you are struggling with living a life that you know is not pleasing to God, write out why. Pray to God on what is causing you to continue in sin. Ask God to reveal where your disobedience stems from internally.

The Samaritan woman's problem was not the men she slept with; it was her worship relationship with God. She had deep-routed internal issues that she was struggling with.

The woman's testimony was strong enough to get a whole city saved. Are you witnessing to people about your God? Has someone else accepted Jesus Christ as Lord and Savior because of your testimony? If not, pray to God to give you boldness to speak to others about the things that He has done for you.

Chapter 28

Mary

Lazarus' Sister

**Mary's act of intercession was
displaying her offer of sacrifice in honor of Jesus.**

Mary
Lazarus' Sister

Six days before the Passover, Jesus came to Bethany, where Laza-
rus lived, whom Jesus had raised from the dead. Here a dinner was
given in Jesus' honor. Martha served, while Lazarus was among
those reclining at the table with him. Then Mary took about a pint
of pure nard, an expensive perfume; she poured it on Jesus' feet
and wiped his feet with her hair. And the house was filled with the
fragrance of the perfume.

"Leave her alone," Jesus replied. "It was intended that she should
save this perfume for the day of my burial (John 12:1-3, 7).

Mary, her sister Martha, and her brother Lazarus were all
friends of Jesus'. They were in the town of Bethany having
a dinner in honor of Jesus. Jesus' disciples were also present at the dinner, which took place several days before Jesus
would to be crucified.

During the dinner celebration, Mary decided to pour out a
very expensive bottle of perfume on Jesus' feet and wipe his
feet with her hair. Due to her act of reverence, some of the
disciples spoke negatively about what she had just done. Jesus told them to leave her alone.

She and her siblings had previously spent quality time with
him. Jesus had dinner with her family before, and during
those times they were able to sit and listen to the words

of Jesus Christ. Mary had personally witnessed Jesus raise her brother from the dead. She had even seen Jesus cry. She knew the calling on his life and that he was more than just a man; he was God in the flesh. She had a personal relationship with Jesus.

Jesus stopped by the city of Bethany on his way to Jerusalem. This was going to be the last visit with Mary and her family before he went to the cross. Could you imagine the emotions that Mary was feeling at this moment? She was at a celebration for her friend who was about to die. Everyone was eating and enjoying themselves not realizing the ultimate sacrifice that Jesus was about give.

Jesus had mentioned to the disciples several times throughout his ministry that he was going to die and rise again. But their focus at this time was not on him, but themselves. Mary however, wanted to acknowledge the man of the hour, her friend Jesus the Christ. Her love and reverence for him drove her to sacrifice something that was monetarily very expensive. It was a bottle of perfume that was valued at one year worth of earnings.

She poured it out on his feet and wiped it with her hair. The disciples thought that she was stupid for doing this. Judas even stated that she could have given that money to the poor. What they did not realize is that they were looking at her carnally; they could not see that she was worshipping Jesus through her sacrifice of her oil. Her sacrifice displayed that nothing in this world was more valuable than the sacrifice Jesus was about to make. Her wiping Jesus' feet with her hair symbolized her positioning toward him—bowing to get to his feet.

Therefore, God exalted him to the highest place and gave him the name that is above every name, that at the name of Jesus every knee should bow, in heaven and on earth and under the earth, and every tongue acknowledge that Jesus Christ is Lord, to the glory of God the Father (Philippians 2:9-11).

Mary bowing down to Jesus displayed her acknowledgment of him as Lord. She was worshipping him. Jesus, unlike his disciples, could see her worship and because of it he rebuked the disciples for criticizing her. He knew that she recognized that he was about to make the ultimate sacrifice.

Application, Thoughts & Questions

Application

Reflect and write about your friendship / relationship with Jesus.

_____
_____
_____
_____
_____

Questions

1. Have you realized the ultimate sacrifice that Jesus made for you? If so, explain below:

_____
_____
_____
_____
_____

If you were not able to answer the question above please read these few scriptures:

John 3:16- _For God so loved the world that he gave his one and only Son, that whoever believes in him shall not perish but have eternal life._

Romans 10:8-13- _But what does it say? "The word is near you; it is in your mouth and in your heart," that is, the message concerning faith that we proclaim: If you declare with your mouth, "Jesus is Lord," and believe in your heart that God raised him from the dead, you will be saved. For it is with your heart that you believe and are justified, and it is with your mouth that you profess your faith and are saved._

As Scripture says, "Anyone who believes in him will never be put to shame." For there is no difference between Jew and Gentile—the same Lord is Lord of all and richly blesses all who call on him, for, "Everyone who calls on the name of the Lord will be saved."

2. Salvation is available to you today. All you need to do is believe with your heart and confess with your mouth that God raised Jesus Christ from the dead for our sins and by faith in your belief of that you are saved. Mary worshipped Jesus despite of who was watching. People or things should never get in the way of your personal relationship with Jesus Christ. Is there anything or person that is hindering your worship today?

_____
_____
_____
_____
_____
_____

3. Mary was willing to sacrifice something that was very valuable to her for Jesus Christ. Is there some thing that you have of value that you are willing to give to Jesus? Monetary things are not always the answer for sacrifice. Gifts and talents are given to all us to edify the body of Christ. Are you sharing the gifts and talents that God has given you to glorify His Kingdom? If not what is hindering you from doing so?

_____
_____
_____
_____
_____

4. Jesus advocated for Mary because of her sacrifice and worship. When the disciples started to complain about what she had done, Jesus immediately came to her defense, and he will do the same for you. What things do you need Jesus to advocate for you today? Write them out and begin to worship him for who He is in your life.

_____
_____
_____
_____
_____

_____
_____
_____
_____
_____
_____

Chapter 29

Mary Magdalene

Mary Magdalene's act of intercession was going to tell the disciples that Jesus had risen.

Mary Magdalene

Now Mary stood outside the tomb crying. As she wept, she bent over to look into the tomb and saw two angels in white, seated where Jesus' body had been, one at the head and the other at the foot.

They asked her, "Woman, why are you crying?"

"They have taken my Lord away," she said, "and I don't know where they have put him." At this, she turned around and saw Jesus standing there, but she did not realize that it was Jesus.

He asked her, "Woman, why are you crying? Who is it you are looking for?"

Thinking he was the gardener, she said, "Sir, if you have carried him away, tell me where you have put him, and I will get him."

Jesus said to her, "Mary."

She turned toward him and cried out in Aramaic, "Rabboni!" (which means "Teacher").

Jesus said, "Do not hold on to me, for I have not yet ascended to the Father. Go instead to my brothers and tell them, 'I am ascending to my Father and your Father, to my God and your God.'"

Mary Magdalene went to the disciples with the news: "I have seen the Lord!" And she told them that he had said these things to her (John 20 11-18).

Acts of Intercession

Mary Magdalene was a devout follower of Jesus Christ before and after his death and resurrection. She came to know him because he had cast out seven demons that were in her. She, along with other women, contributed their time and money to Jesus and his disciples. She had not only been a follower of Jesus Christ, but she also witnessed his death and burial.

Witnessing Jesus' death on the cross must have been very traumatizing for those like Mary, whose lives were transformed by him. He had been beaten and mistreated the day before he had to carry the cross that he would be nailed to by Roman soldiers. He also had a crown of thrones placed in his skull. From the beatings, mistreatment, and head trauma, his body was bloody and bruised.

While Jesus was hanging on the cross for many hours, people mocked him, soldiers gambled for his clothing and the man hanging on the cross next to him told him to save himself. Religious leaders ridiculed him. When Jesus died the sky became as night and the earth quaked. Mary Magdalene was present to see it all.

Can you imagine the feelings and emotions Mary was dealing with? Jesus had changed her life. She had witnessed the many miracles he performed of healing and deliverance. She had sat under his teachings and he was her teacher. Now she had to witness this man of greatness be crucified. Mary witnessing these events led her into severe grief.

Grief is a natural emotion to experience right after the death of a loved one. It is hard to accept death; it is even harder to witness death. Mary Magdalene's grief had gripped her to the point that when she was in the presence of angels and Jesus in the tomb, she could not recognize them for who they were. She was so consumed with grief that she was not able to see the truth when it was right in front of her. The angels were dressed in white and they were speaking to her. In her grief she did not recognized that she was in the presence of angels. She did the same with Jesus. She did not recognize she was speaking with him until he called her name. Once He called her name she was able to see Jesus.

When we face difficult times in our lives such as grief, pain, coping with a loss, unbearable pain, etc., we need to be able to hear a Word from the Lord. Jesus did not just speak any words, he called out *her* name. When Jesus calls *our* names, he is speaking to us from the position of Lord, Savior, Redeemer, Deliverer, Sustainer, Father, Teacher, Provider, Comforter and Creator.

Now that Jesus has risen from the dead, he calls our names from an internal place called Everlasting life. Where Jesus abides, there is no suffering, death, disappointments, or sin; Jesus' death brings life to us. The last time Mary had seen Jesus and heard his voice he was dying on the cross.

Jesus may have looked and sounded differently because on the cross he was carrying the sins of the world. When Mary saw Jesus, he did not look like what he had been through. His body was very bloody on the cross, but when Mary saw him, his body was restored. His death and resurrection is the hope we have when we are dealing with the problems of life. He is living proof that there is life after death. He is the one who died for our sins and rose from the dead so we may have eternal life.

Also, his resurrection represents what He is able to do in our seemingly dead situations. Mary's grief had her accepting death as the final answer for Jesus. Jesus was able to prove grief wrong. He is able to resurrect any bad situation in our life. Whatever we are facing that seems hopeless and desolate remember that Jesus is able to bring restoration to it.

When Jesus called Mary Magdalene she responded to him as Teacher. Her response indicated who He was in her life. Jesus was able to teach her the things of God and His Kingdom. She was able to see that Jesus did not change who he was before the crucifixion.

People may change, but God's Word does not. The Word of God is the most consistent thing we have to rely on in our life. Jesus standing right in front of Mary symbolized his teachings manifested in her life. His very presence is a lesson for all of us. When we accept Jesus Christ as our Lord and Savior he seals us with his Holy Spirit. His Holy Spirit resides in us and He instructs us according to God's Word. God is always present in our lives, but how do we respond when he speaks to us?

Jesus gave Mary specific instructions after he had her undivided attention. He told her not to embrace him, because he has not yet ascended to the Father. He told her to go and tell the disciples that He had risen. Mary went immediately and did what He told her to do.

When God speaks to us and gives us something to do, we must act on it immediately. When Jesus shows up in your life, it is not for you to keep to yourself. Others need to know about the death and resurrection of Jesus Christ. Jesus' presence was able to bring Mary out of her grief. She understood that the disciples needed to have the same experience that she had. There are people God has placed in our lives who need to hear about what He has done for us. They need to hear the Savior of the world has risen from the dead with all power in his hands, and our belief in Him has brought us salvation.

Application, Thoughts & Questions

Application

If you are grief stricken, keep seeking Jesus. Mary did and she found him. He spoke a word to her and it changed her state of mind. Jesus is able to heal the deepest pain we have.

He knows what it is like to go through pain, because of what He endured on the cross. He loves you and wants you to be able to enjoy this life here on earth and the life to come after death. Do you believe in Jesus Christ more than your current situation?

Questions

1. What things in your life need resurrecting?

_____

_____

_____

_____

2. Mary Magdalene was healed from seven demons, and she also was healed from grief. Jesus was not just her Teacher; he was her Savior and Lord. What has Jesus healed you from?

_____

_____

_____

_____

3. What has Jesus told you to do that you have not done yet, and what is holding you back?

_____

_____

_____

_____

_____

Chapter 30

Rhoda

Rhoda's act of intercession was testifying to
answered prayer (Peter) despite disbelief.

Rhoda

When this had dawned on him, he went to the house of Mary the mother of John, also called Mark, where many people had gathered and were praying. Peter knocked at the outer entrance and a servant named Rhoda came to answer the door. When she recognized Peter's voice, she was so overjoyed she ran back without opening it and exclaimed, "Peter is at the door!"

"You're out of your mind," they told her. When she kept insisting that it was so, they said, "It must be his angel."

But, Peter kept on knocking, and when they opened the door and saw him, they were astonished. Peter motioned with his hand for them to be quiet and described how the Lord had brought him out of prison. "Tell James and the other brothers and sisters about this," he said, and then he left for another place (Acts 12:12-17).

The early church had just formed in Jerusalem, and members were undergoing persecution from their opposition. Peter the apostle had been arrested for spreading the gospel of Jesus Christ. He had just supernaturally escaped from prison and went to the house of Mary, where her and other believers were praying for his release.

When Peter knocked at the door, the servant Rhoda heard his voice and went back and told everyone that Peter was at the door. Nobody believed her, but she insisted he was there. Peter kept knocking and when everyone came to the door, opened it, and saw Peter they were astonished.

Acts of Intercession

The Book of Acts is about the acts of the Holy Ghost manifesting in the early church. The gospel of Jesus Christ was spreading quickly in the city of Jerusalem, and thousands of people were converting to Christianity. With the growth of the church came persecution of believers–especially the ones spreading the gospel.

Peter was very instrumental in the growth of the new church. Thousands of people were saved because of one of his messages. Government officials and the religious leaders in the city instructed him to stop preaching the message of Christ. Peter refused to keep silent about the message of Jesus Christ and because of it he was imprisoned. The believers were at Mary's house praying mightily for Peter's release from prison and their request was answered while they were still praying. The supernatural works of the Holy Ghost had manifested instantaneously through their prayer.

When Rhoda answered the door and heard Peter, she told those in the house. They did not believe it. We can make the same mistakes that the believers did by praying without expecting God to answer. God answered them while they were praying, but because it came from Rhoda, a servant girl, they didn't believe her.

Thank goodness Rhoda stood firm on what she knew for herself. She insisted they come to the door with her and they found that Rhoda was correct all along. We cannot become so spiritual that we miss God. God can use anyone to deliver a message from Him. The next time you pray make sure you are anticipating God to answer you. The message may not come the way you think it should, but it will come.

Don't allow others to make you believe that you are out of your mind when it comes to what you have seen God do in your life. Rhoda was a servant and she was probably looked down upon as not being a creditable witness because of her status.

You may not have a big fancy title, education, high income, pray like a warrior, or know the Bible word-for-word. But, if you know what God has done for you, never let your status stop your witness for Christ. God is not impressed by our prayers. What moves Him is our faith behind the prayers.

Rhoda's response when she heard Peter at the door was joy, so much so that she forgot to open it. She ran back in the house to tell the others he was here. When you are filled with joy, it should make you want to share it with others so they can experience the same thing. Her intentions were to let the others know that God had answered their prayers. She wanted them to know that it was time to stop praying and time to start praising God for what he had done.

Prayer and praise go great together. When you pray you are asking for a specific request from God. When you praise, after you have prayed, you are acknowledging that God's will is already done in your life. He will answer you according to His Word. It may not come when you think it should, but He will always bring it on time. Some prayer requests will be answered immediately, like in Peter's case. Other request may take time to reveal. Whatever the case may be, keep seeking God until you receive your answer.

Application, Thoughts & Questions

Application

Look back over the things you have been praying for and begin to praise God for the victory that you have through his son Christ Jesus.

Questions

1. Who have you been praying for and what results are you expecting?

_____
_____
_____
_____
_____
_____

2. Have you even shared a testimony with some one and they did not believe you? How did it make you feel or what was your response?

_____
_____
_____
_____
_____
_____

Chapter 31
Lydia

Lydia's act of intercession was becoming one of the first converts in Philippi and helping aid in the ministry of Paul and Silas.

Lydia

From there we traveled to Philippi, a Roman colony and the leading city of that district of Macedonia. And we stayed there several days.

On the Sabbath we went outside the city gate to the river, where we expected to find a place of prayer. We sat down and began to speak to the women who had gathered there. One of those listening was a woman from the city of Thyatira named Lydia, a dealer in purple cloth. She was a worshiper of God.

The Lord opened her heart to respond to Paul's message. When she and the members of her household were baptized, she invited us to her home.

"If you consider me a believer in the Lord," she said, "come and stay at my house." And she persuaded us.

After Paul and Silas came out of the prison, they went to Lydia's house, where they met with the brothers and sisters and encouraged them. Then they left (Acts 16:12-15, 40).

Lydia met Paul and Silas at the river and heard the message of Christ. She immediately believed and her and her household were saved. She was a woman of wealth and she help to aid Paul and Silas missionary trips. She was instrumental in founding the church of Philippi.

Lydia was a Gentile who worshipped the God of Israel. The message of Christ had not come to her region until Paul and

Silas arrived. The day she met Paul and Silas and heard their message was the day her life changed. She and her family accepted Jesus as their Lord and Savior and they all were baptized.

She invited Paul and Silas to stay at her home during their stay. She and her family were one of the first converts in the land of Philippi. When Paul and Silas were released from prison, they went to Lydia's house and encouraged the new converted believers and left for another mission trip.

Lydia was a woman of influence. When she converted to Christianity so did the members of her family. Their conversion was the start of the church in Philippi. The message they carried about Jesus Christ was contagious because the church grew in Philippi. Paul's letter of encouragement to the Philippians is found in the new testament of the Bible.

Lydia sold purple cloth; and in those days that equated to wealth. She could have let her wealth get in the way of her worship of God. Instead, she chose to use her wealth to help aid in the ministry of Paul and Silas. She did not use her influence for selfish gain; rather she used it to bring others into the Kingdom of God.

We can use our influence of wealth and prestige to bring others into the Kingdom of God. God blesses us so we can be a blessing to others. Lydia wanted to bless the men who were carrying the message of Christ. She understood how important this message of salvation was and she wanted to participate in the spreading of it locally in Philippi and worldwide through Paul and Silas's ministry.

Application, Thoughts & Questions

Thought

How many people have accepted Jesus Christ as their Lord and Savior since you have been converted? If none, pray to God to give you boldness to speak to others about Christ.

Questions

1. The gospel changed Lydia's life and she responded by sharing the good news, and supporting the ministry. How has the gospel changed your life and what is your response to it?

_____
_____
_____
_____
_____
_____

2. What is holding you back from giving to your local church and/or giving to any ministry spreading the gospel of Jesus Christ? Do you see how your giving is connected to the salvation of others?

_____
_____
_____
_____
_____
_____

Chapter 32
Aquila & Priscilla

Aquila and Priscilla's act of intercession was using their marriage ministry to grow the church.

Aquila & Priscilla

After this, Paul left Athens and went to Corinth. There he met a Jew named Aquila, a native of Pontus, who had recently come from Italy with his wife Priscilla, because Claudius had ordered all Jews to leave Rome. Paul went to see them, and because he was a tentmaker as they were, he stayed and worked with them.

Paul stayed on in Corinth for some time. Then he left the brothers and sisters and sailed for Syria, accompanied by Priscilla and Aquila. Before he sailed, he had his hair cut off at Cenchreae because of a vow he had taken.

Meanwhile a Jew named Apollos, a native of Alexandria, came to Ephesus. He was a learned man, with a thorough knowledge of the Scriptures. He had been instructed in the way of the Lord, and he spoke with great fervor and taught about Jesus accurately, though he knew only the baptism of John. He began to speak boldly in the synagogue. When Priscilla and Aquila heard him, they invited him to their home and explained to him the way of God more adequately (Acts 18:1-3, 18, 24- 26, Rom. 16:3-5, 1 Cor. 16:19).

Greet Priscilla and Aquila, my co-workers in Christ Jesus. They risked their lives for me. Not only I but all the churches of the Gentiles are grateful to them. Greet also the church that meets at their house. Greet my dear friend Epenetus, who was the first convert to Christ in the province of Asia (Rom. 16:3-5).

The churches in the province of Asia send you greetings. Aquila and Priscilla greet you warmly in the Lord, and so does the church that meets at their house (1 Cor. 16:19).

Acts of Intercession

Aquila and Priscilla were husband and wife who were followers of Jesus Christ. Paul was in their city of Corinth doing missionary work for quite some time. He ended up living and working with them as tent makers. When Paul left and sailed for Syria on another missionary trip, Aquila and Priscilla went with him.

They were able to help spread the ministry of the Gospel of Christ with Paul. They taught the word and even held church services in their home. Aquila, Priscilla, and Paul were not only friends they were co-workers in the tent making business and the spreading of the Gospel of Jesus Christ.

How can your marriage be a ministry? It is a ministry when the husband and the wife realize that God brought them together to grow His Kingdom. Aquila and Priscilla's names are never mentioned separately in the scriptures; they worked together as one unit. Both of them were Jews who converted to Christianity.

They lived and worked with Paul for a long period of time and they were able to grow in the Word of God through Paul's teachings and ministry. The tent-making business was a mobile business, meaning they could travel and still make a living on the road. When it was time for Paul to leave and go to Syria, Aquila and Priscilla went with him.

One specific accomplishment they achieved together (separate from Paul) was that they were able to correct Apollo's teachings of Jesus to others. Apollo was a believer and preacher of Jesus, but he had only heard the teachings of John the Baptist. He did not know that Jesus had died and rose again for the salvation of the world.

Aquila and Priscilla knew it was imperative that Apollo be made aware of Jesus, so he could be a more effective and accurate preacher. They invited him to their home to talk with him about the message he was preaching. Inviting Apollo to their home was a wise decision because it made the approach welcoming and sentimental.

Wisdom is a great tool to use when correcting someone in error. Apollo was an educated man and a great speaker, but he lacked important information. Apollo accepted their teaching and he left their home better equipped to preach the word of God.

The next time you need to mentor someone about their lack of knowledge, ask God to give you wisdom with your approach. You want your message to be effective and to be received in a non-threatening way. They also used their home as a gathering place for teaching and worship (church) in the cities of Ephesus, and Rome. Their skillful trade of tent making blessed them to be able to travel, make a good living, and spread the gospel of Christ. They used what God blessed them with (gifts and talents) to help grow the church throughout the region.

Application, Thoughts & Questions

Application
Are you currently working with others in the ministry of Christ? If not, pray for God to divinely connect to the place/people where you need to be.

Paul was not only Aquila and Priscilla's friend, he was a mentor in the Gospel of Christ. Who are some mentors who you have in the body of Christ? If you do not have any, pray to God to send a mentor in your life.

Questions
1. Has God used your gifts and talents to bless the body of Christ? How?

_____
_____
_____
_____

2. Aquila and Priscilla's home was used as a place where people could come and learn about the word of God. What do people learn about God when they come to your house?

_____
_____
_____
_____

3. Aquila and Priscilla were on one accord in their marriage. How are you and your spouse operating together in the gifting and talents that God has blessed you with to grow His Kingdom?

_____
_____
_____
_____

Chapter 33
Phoebe

Phoebe's act of intercession was her leadership as a deaconess in her local church.

Phoebe

I commend to you our sister Phoebe, a deacon of the church in Cenchreae. I ask you to receive her in the Lord in a way worthy of his people and to give her any help she may need from you, for she has been the benefactor of many people, including me (Romans 16:1-2).

This is the only mention of Phoebe in the Bible but it speaks volumes. Phoebe was a deaconess of the church in Cenchreae. Paul was acknowledging her character and leadership role in the church. She was a servant leader that gave to Paul's ministry and other ministries through her service and finances.

1 Timothy 3:8-13 gives a biblical description/qualifications of a deacon. In the same way, deacons are to be worthy of respect, sincere, not indulging in much wine, and not pursuing dishonest gain. They must keep hold of the deep truths of the faith with a clear conscience. They must first be tested; and then if there is nothing against them, let them serve as deacons. In the same way, the women are to be worthy of respect, not malicious talkers but temperate and trustworthy in everything.

A deacon must be faithful to his wife and must manage his children and his household well. Those who have served well gain an excellent standing and great assurance in their faith in Christ Jesus. To be recognized by the Apostle Paul as a deaconess in the church was a great honor for Phoebe.

Acts of Intercession

Paul was instrumental in getting the message of the Gospel out to the Gentiles. He had helped start various churches throughout the region. Along the way, Paul met many people who helped him achieve and continue the work that he was sent to do.

In Romans 16, he was giving thanks to all his co-workers and friends who helped him along the way of his journey. Paul was grateful for Phoebe's faithfulness to the ministry. He wanted to publicly acknowledge her work and service to his ministry and the local church. He wanted the people of Cenchreae to have the same esteem for her as he did.

Recognition from influential men and women is great, but recognition from God is better. Phoebe was faithful in her calling as a deaconess and because of it God showed her favor through Paul's acknowledgement. It is one thing to have a title in the church and it is another thing to live out your title. God looks beyond the titles given to us by man; instead He looks at our faithfulness and service unto Him.

1 Timothy 3:8-13 (Amplified version) gives instruction/qualifications on how a deacon/deaconess should live their lives. Yet the principles can also apply to all believers in Christ. They are:

a)   Worthy of respect,

b)   Not shifty and double talkers but sincere in what they say,

c)   Not drinking much wine,

d)   Not pursuing dishonest gain (craving wealth and resorting to ignoble and dishonest methods of getting it);

e)   Possess the mystic secret of faith (Christian

truth as hidden from ungodly men) with a
clear conscience,

f)   Are tried and investigated and proved first;
then if they turn out to be above reproach,
let them serve (as deacons);

g)   The women likewise must be worthy of
respect and serious, not gossipers, but temperate and self-controlled, (thoroughly)
trustworthy in all things, and

h)   Let deacons be the husbands of but one
wife, and let them manage their children
and their own households well.

The difference between a deacon/deaconess and a regular
church member is that they are more accountable for their actions. They should be mature in their faith walk with Christ.
They are to serve others in the church and assist the pastor
with the growth of the local church.

Phoebe assisted Paul in his ministry and she possessed the
qualities of a deaconess through her service at her local
church. Whether or not we have the title of a deacon or deaconess in our church, we can still chose to serve God and his
people through our actions. There is a place for all of Christ's
believers to serve in the local and global body. The most important lesson we can gain from Phoebe is to be faithful in
whatever God has for you to do in the church. God will bless
you as you continue to work for Him.

Application, Thoughts & Questions

Questions

1. What things have you been faithful over? How have you experienced God's favor in your life?

_____

_____

_____

_____

_____

_____

_____

2. What is your role in ministry at your local church? If you are not active in ministry, pray to God to lead you in the area where He wants you to serve.

_____

_____

_____

_____

_____

_____

Final Remarks

My prayer is that you saw yourself in these various women of the Bible. These women's lives reflect the Living Word God has placed in all of us. God can use any situation, circumstance, person, place, thing, past, present, and future to get His will accomplished in earth.

We are the ones who "stand in the gap" between the destiny of ourselves, and the ones who are coming after us. Nothing we have experienced will go to waste as it relates to the will of God.

Romans 8:28 states: *And we know in all things God works for the good of those who love him, who have been called according to his purpose.*

God has a purpose for all of us, and we will discover what it is as we stay in His Word. Do not let this book be the last stop in your quest of seeking God's will for your life. Stay connected to His Word and Christ church for your continual development in Him.

Prayer

Shana Wise

Father God, I thank you for choosing us when we did not choose you and ordaining us to bear fruit that will remain. I thank you for your Son who sits at your right hand interceding on our behalf.

I thank you for Your Holy Spirit that leads and guides us into all truth. I thank you for everyone who reads this book. I thank you for changing their lives through your Word. I thank you for the ones who will come to know Christ as their Lord and Savior.

I thank you for all the answers you have provided through your Word. I praise you for the great and mighty things you are going to do in the lives of those who have decided to make a change according to your Word. All the glory, honor, and power belong to you. In your son Jesus name.

Amen

About the Author

Shana Wise

Shana Wise currently serves an associate minister at Christian Leaders Fellowship in Jacksonville, Florida. She was licensed as a minister in 2013, and as an elder in 2014.

In addition to her nearly 20 years experience working in ministry, Shana is the CEO of 1 Wise Choice Inc., in partnership with her husband Beauron.

She is a nurse, actress/model, preacher, prayer warrior, mentor and motivational speaker. She and her husband, Beauron, are the parents of Imani, Justin, Chris and Devon.

For speaking engagements or bulk book sale rates contact: wisechoiceinc@gmail.com.